# Mindfulness and Meditation

Beginner's Meditation Guide to Eliminate Stress, Anxiety and Depression

(Ultimate Guide to Achieve Happiness by Eliminating Stress)

**David McCoy**

Published by Rob Miles

© **David McCoy**

All Rights Reserved

*Mindfulness and Meditation: Beginner's Meditation Guide to Eliminate Stress, Anxiety and Depression (Ultimate Guide to Achieve Happiness by Eliminating Stress)*

ISBN 978-1-990084-03-4

All rights reserved. No part of this guide may be reproduced in any form without permission in writing from the publisher except in the case of brief quotations embodied in critical articles or reviews.

## LEGAL & DISCLAIMER

The information contained in this book is not designed to replace or take the place of any form of medicine or professional medical advice. The information in this book has been provided for educational and entertainment purposes only.

The information contained in this book has been compiled from sources deemed reliable, and it is accurate to the best of the Author's knowledge; however, the Author cannot guarantee its accuracy and validity and cannot be held liable for any errors or omissions. Changes are periodically made to this book. You must consult your doctor or get professional medical advice before using any of the suggested remedies, techniques, or information in this book.

Upon using the information contained in this book, you agree to hold harmless the Author from and against any damages, costs, and expenses, including any legal fees potentially resulting from the application of any of the information provided by this guide. This disclaimer applies to any damages or injury caused by the use and application, whether directly or indirectly, of any advice or information presented, whether for breach of contract, tort, negligence, personal injury, criminal intent, or under any other cause of action.

You agree to accept all risks of using the information presented inside this book. You need to consult a professional medical practitioner in order to ensure you are both able and healthy enough to participate in this program.

# Table of Contents

INTRODUCTION .................................................................. 1

CHAPTER 1: THE MIND ....................................................... 3

CHAPTER 2: MINDFULNESS MEDITATION: GETTING STARTED.......................................................................... 8

CHAPTER 3: ACHIEVE MINDFULNESS THROUGH MINDFUL MEDITATION ................................................................... 13

CHAPTER 4: FORGIVENESS AND PERSONAL STRENGTHS.. 20

CHAPTER 4: WHY SHOULD YOU USE MINDFULNESS? ...... 24

CHAPTER 5: WHAT IS MINDFULNESS? ............................. 32

CHAPTER 6: CONSCIOUSLY CHOOSE AWARENESS ........... 46

CHAPTER 7: IMPROVING YOUR PRACTICE ....................... 50

CHAPTER 8: DEPRESSION ................................................. 54

CHAPTER 9: DEEPER EXERCISES ....................................... 61

CHAPTER 10: HEALTHY MINDFULNESS ATTITUDES .......... 68

CHAPTER 11: HOW TO MEDITATE .................................... 82

CHAPTER 12: MINDFULNESS MEDITATION AND HEALTH BENEFITS .......................................................................... 94

CHAPTER 13: MINDFULNESS? YES PLEASE! ................... 105

CHAPTER 14: HOW MINDFULNESS HELPS EASE STRESS . 111

CHAPTER 15: MEDITATION AND MINDFULNESS ............ 115

CHAPTER 16: AS A MAN (OR WOMAN) THINKETH… ...... 134

**CHAPTER 17: MINDFULNESS EXERCISES FOR BEGINNERS ................................................................ 140**

**CHAPTER 18: TECHNIQUES OF TRANSCENDENTAL MEDITATION ................................................................ 144**

**CHAPTER 19: PRACTISING BODY SCAN .......................... 155**

**CHAPTER 20: MINDFULNESS TECHNIQUES .................... 163**

**CHAPTER 21: CREATIVITY .............................................. 172**

**CHAPTER 22: THE POWER OF POSITIVITY ...................... 177**

**CHAPTER 23: OVERCOMING PERFECTIONISM ................ 182**

**CHAPTER 24: LEARNING MINDFULNESS MEDITATION ... 189**

**CHAPTER 25: MAINTAINING MINDFULNESS .................. 196**

**CONCLUSION ................................................................ 202**

## Introduction

Although one might associate the word "mindfulness" with being alert and that may not sit well with those who see meditation as being calm, the two do go hand in hand because you can indeed be mindful and be at peace with the world. Mindful meditation is slightly different from that practiced by yoga experts, though Buddhist monks are very aware of their surroundings as well as extremely aware of themselves and are able to balance the two elements very well indeed. The sense of well-being that you are able to glean from mindfulness is extremely powerful, in that it opens up a whole new world of understanding and energy that comes from within you.

Walk through the pages of this book to gain a greater understanding of yourself and your surroundings and, in doing so, learn how to relax and to use that relaxation to improve the way that you react with the world around you. It will make you a happier person who is much more able to cope with the stresses of life because of the new-found calmness.

This book explains the process, and takes you into the way that mindfulness meditation can make you see life from another perspective. That perspective is more balanced, more able to appreciate and more able to feel at one with nature, the world around you and those people who cross the path of your life. It's a valuable lesson to learn. Once you do, you will find life takes on a whole new perspective.

## Chapter 1: The Mind

Many have argued that the concept of mind is rather a very abstract debate. This discussion becomes very cumbersome to explain because the mind is not a physical object that can be seen, touched or felt. For these reasons, the mind has been considered not to be part of the human body because there is no blood in it, it cannot feel pain nor can it be repaired through medical surgery.

What then is the Mind? The mind can be considered to be the thinking part of a human psychological setup that accounts for human consciousness and reflections, hence its abstract nature. However, it has been confused to be or work as part of the human brain because it deals with consciousness and reflections which some have interpreted to be thinking, which is the sole responsibility of the brain. However, as explained earlier, the mind is invisible and cannot be found in human body if dissected. However, the brain is part of a human body system; it can get damaged and can be fixed through a medical surgery, it could be seen when the human body is dissected and even taken out of body, and therefore can be touched.

It will therefore be appropriate to say from the foregoing that, the mind is the base of human perception and cognition that aids a human person to appreciate the things he hears, sees and feels. The mind is the starting point of every human actions, feelings and thoughts. The great philosopher Aristotle considers mind to be part of the human soul by which it knows and understands. He sees mind as the part of human intellect that helps man to understand things. The mind is therefore the experience that a human person has in him or herself. Such experiences include thoughts, consciousness, memories, emotions, beliefs, sensations, or even desires, among others.

Just as sensual capabilities is very vital to an animal, the mind is as important to a human person. This is because all the experience listed takes place in a human body. The mind, body and the brain work together in unison to help man to appreciate each and every experience that he is faced with. For instance, the testosterone in the human body accounts for the competiveness of man, the hormones that are distributed in the human body accounts for emotions and thoughts of man, and the adrenalin in the human body supports energy or anxiety in man. Also, the immune system responds to psychological stress to influence the mood of man, and the brain makes use of bodily activities (such as movement of muscles, breathing and postures etc.) to understand what the self-image and the emotional state of humans is. This means that in conjunction with the human body and brain, the mind does more than reflection, consciousness and understanding. It aids a human person to deliberate on, strategize, plan and decide on a course of action.

To this end, Aristotle divided mind into two basic units- the theoretical mind and the practical. The theoretical mind deals with the imaginary or abstract part of intellect and reason that says that mind is not part of a human body as it cannot be seen, felt or touched, but it is intuitive, subliminal, conscious or subconscious and hidden in the soul and body of every human person. The practical mind, on the other hand deals majorly with an applied part of intellect and reason which is aided by the brain.

It will therefore be safe to deduce from the foregoing that the mind is that conscious think feeling that a human person experiences from time to time in relation to any activity or expression of man. This conscious feeling has taken over the personality of "I" which operates with an audible voice within a human person and serves as a causal driving force for all actions and inactions of a human person. The conscious think feeling also as understood, relates to the brain and body in one way or another, even though it is apparently separate, not being part of the human brain or body. The mind is that voice you hear when you read a novel or a textbook to yourself silently (the brain at this point processes the information taking in), it is the voice that helps you to ponder on situations and make up your mind on the next line of action to take.

## Chapter 2: Mindfulness Meditation: Getting Started

There are mindfulness books that you can find and even videos over at the internet that can be helpful. This book also has the information you need to practice and master mindfulness.

The practice of mindfulness can be done through meditation and yoga. This book will give you mindfulness meditation techniques and strategies to get you started. Even as a beginner, you there is nothing to worry about since you the guides in the succeeding chapters are easy to follow and understand.

What is Mindfulness Meditation?

Meditation is the practice of training your mind to achieve clarity by directing your thoughts and focus to a single object. Living in this fast phased world makes it difficult for anybody to sit for even 5 minutes and think of nothing, let alone spending 30 minutes of meditation. But the easiest way to begin meditating is to focus on your breathing.

Concentration Meditation

Concentration meditation technique focuses on a single point: like being aware of your breath, reciting a word or mantra over and over, listening to a repetitive sound, or staring at a candle flame or any object at hand. This type of meditation lets you refocus your awareness on one particular object that you have chosen. Instead of pursuing random thoughts, this technique helps you to let go of these random thoughts, thus allowing you to concentrate on the task at one.

Mindfulness Meditation

Mindfulness meditation on the other hand, allows you to observe your thoughts and feelings and how they move in specific patterns. With constant practice, inner balance is likely to develop.

Mindfulness is something that each one of us has, but most of us are not aware that we have it and how it we can further develop it. It is a non-judgmental, inviting whatever comes, friendly, and openhearted kind of awareness. You cultivate it by deeply paying attention on purpose, without clouding your mind with any form of judgment to whatever may happen at that particular moment.

Mindfulness lifts you from the "autopilot" mode of living your life and lets you live life fully by focusing on the present moment.

How often should You Practice Mindfulness Meditation Techniques?

Ideally, you have to practice every day so you can easily develop a sense of stability and inner calmness. It also allows you to develop non-reactivity of the mind, thus allowing you to embrace whatever events may happen to you during the day, whether pleasant or unpleasant. This in turn helps you to be more compassionate to others.

Practicing daily helps you to learn how to detach yourself from habitual thoughts, emotions, and behaviors that hinder you from connecting with your inner self and with others in a deeper and healthier way.

While it is natural for us, humans, for our minds to wander most of the time, we also have the power to refocus. People often get lost in thoughts of the future or of the past, and they miss enjoying every moment that they got, until that present moment also becomes another memory of the past.

Distractions in your daily mindfulness life can produce worry, fear, stress, and anxiety, among other negative emotions that only bring us down. But with the regular practice of mindfulness meditation, you can refocus on the now and learn to actually live in the moment.

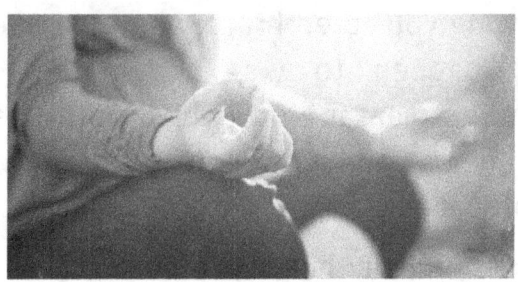

How Should You Practice?

The techniques will help you to become fully aware of the present moment. It is similar to practicing your piano skills every day, you practice being mindful through meditation. You will use your breath as the object to focus on for awareness. You will follow the physical sensations of your breathing, as it comes in and out of your body. You will let your breathing to flow naturally, without having to control or force it to. You only hold the sensation of every breath in your field of awareness.

## Chapter 3: Achieve Mindfulness Through Mindful Meditation

Now some people think that meditation is an act of not thinking anything, that it's about keeping a blank mind. But do you know how difficult that is? How can you possibly not think of anything? Even when your mind is blank, you're still thinking about how to sustain the blankness. While most people will say that you can achieve a thoughtless mind through meditation, I think that, practically speaking, it requires years of practice and lots of time. Deadlines, work pressure, children, diet, health thoughts only come when you don't want them to come. But on the other hand, can you avoid them? Or, should you avoid them? Tricky isn't it?

While I'm not going to tell you what to think and what not to think, simply because only you know the kind of pressure you're going through, I will however give you some breathing space.

Mindful mediation isn't about keeping a blank mind; it's about focusing on a thought, figuring out where you're overdoing it and then setting it aside. For instance, if someone has said something hurtful to you, when it's time to meditate, listen to your thoughts. What made that person say those things to you? Were you at fault? If so, apologize. If you weren't, why even bother worrying about them? Remember that your thoughts have a massive impact on your emotions and the decision you make, which sometimes you might regret.

If you don't want to end up in a situation where you're heard saying, "I made a wrong decision!" you need to focus on your thoughts and solve them calmly instead of pushing yourself too far. But if you don't want to focus on them, if you think they're inevitable, then focus on your breathing, your senses, your body, or anything else that craves your attention. The point is to calm yourself, not to cook up new ideas or schemes, or think about what you should do tomorrow morning! With that in mind, just let go of yourself and bask in the glory of your thoughts and emotions and you'll see how mindful you feel when you're done meditating!

## Figuring Out the Types of Mindful Meditation

If you were to visit a meditation center, you'll be bombarded with the types of mediation available to the average customer. Recently, I went to one and was asked whether I wanted concentration medication, reflective meditation, heart-centered meditation, creative meditation, transcendental meditation, and the list goes on. If I weren't aware of the different types of meditation, I would have just turned red and rushed out of the center!

### Formal Meditation

Formal mediation is when, in 24 hours, you take out some time for yourself to sit down and meditate. It could be any time of the day, any number of minutes, to intentionally focus on your thoughts and understand your mind. This type of meditation deepens your mindfulness practice and allows you to understand the tendencies of your mind, your character and your overall ability to respond to your experience. For example, I take out 30 minutes every day to meditate and focus on things that really require my attention so that I can fully justify my decision/behavior towards it. With formal meditation, you will be able to:

Sleep better

Balance your work and personal life better

Engage in meaningful relationships with yourself and others

Better understand yourself and others

Make better decisions and set realistic expectations

Informal Meditation

Informal meditation is when you're completely focused on what you're doing right now. It could be anything really, all that matters is that you focus 100% on something and don't allow your mind to indirectly stress you on other things. So whether you're driving, cooking, cleaning, working, teaching, learning…anything at all, you continue to focus on your thoughts to deepen your ability to be in the presence of mind instead of day dreaming and/or thinking about something that can wait its turn. With informal meditation, you will be able to:

Be productive at work

Find time for formal meditation

Respond to experiences instead of reacting to them

Do more in less time

Solve problems creatively

Balance your work and personal life

Mindfulness Can Make You a Better Person

We're humans and whether you like it or not, sometimes we will get lost in our thoughts. Most of the day, when we're busy doing something, our mind does something else altogether – it's free to wander and seed as many thoughts as possible. In short, we're operating on automatic pilot mode. During the automatic pilot mode, the pilot can leave his/her seat to do something else; the same goes with our mind. But when it comes to our mind, the story is slightly different. The mind seeds thoughts that are practically unhelpful and sometimes the reason behind it is because, as people today will say, "you're still living in the past."

I'll give you an example. People take a break from their everyday lives and finally go on vacation, but when they're vacationing, they'll still be thinking about what's the first thing they're going to do when they get back home. What does this tell you? No matter where they do, they willingly and unknowingly take stress, depression, and anxiousness with them. But if they practice mindfulness, they'd leave all that behind and live in the present moment, enjoy their lives, and come back rejuvenated. Mindfulness helps you to accept the reality so you can make better decisions when the time comes. It shows you how to embrace your feelings so you never feel edged or reckless. As soon as you accept the reality, thoughts become clearer and less hard on you!

## Chapter 4: Forgiveness And Personal Strengths

Mindfulness has been used in therapy and psychology to improve people's minds. In the '90s, researchers used mindfulness-based therapy in their programs, which were built to help people who were experiencing remission from major depressive disorder. In this study, the participants were to practice meditation (based on mindfulness) for almost an hour each day for two months. They were also instructed to have shorter periods to meditate during the day in order to bring together the formal and informal forms of mindfulness and meditation. They were told about the symptoms and signs of depressive disorder and the way these can be changed when the disorder shifts. They were also given tools for how to prevent relapses into depression and to understand the way thoughts and moods influence and interact with each other.

Mindfulness Method Number Three: Mindfulness and Forgiveness.

When you decide to undertake this journey, you are not going to be perfect at it from the very first day. This is why taking forgiveness into consideration as part of your mindfulness practice is so necessary. Being able to forgive yourself and extend compassion toward your mistakes is an irreplaceable part of self-care. Research shows that practicing self-forgiveness and compassion is healthy for your body and mind. Remember to forgive yourself when any of the following occurs:

Anytime you forget to be mindful.

Anytime you are caught up being busy.

Anytime you miss a meditation.

Anytime your mind will not stop wandering.

Instead of getting caught up on the mistakes you believe you have made, try instead to focus on the positive actions you have taken and your intentions to improve yourself. Any time a difficulty pops up on this journey, see it as a chance to learn, or better yet as something normal and expected.

Mindfulness Method Number Four: Find Your Strengths.

The highest character strengths you have, scientifically referred to as signature strengths, will be the best sources of energy along your mindfulness journey, so be sure to take advantage of this. Whichever your best character qualities are, think about ways that you can use them to help you overcome obstacles to staying mindful.

**Examples of Using Strengths:** You might, for instance, rely on your natural ability to be grateful; anytime your mind begins wandering, by expressing that you are grateful you have an active imagination. If your strength is planning, rely on that strength by figuring out how you will stick to your new meditation schedule. If you are great at being humble, focus on being curious whenever you find that your mind is acting anxious.

**Add it to Meditation:** Whenever you practice your mindfulness meditation next, add your strength to the session and use it to make it even more powerful. As soon as you notice a body or mental obstacle, draw energy from your strong quality. If you can, focus on another character strength for an even better experience.

This technique and the ideas given to you above are meant to bring enthusiasm and energy into your daily practice to keep it lively and interesting. When you think about them, you can access great motivation in your personal strengths, so why not add this to mindfulness to make it even better? This will help you become even more committed to the path because you will get past the obstacles that you previously thought were extremely difficult or even impossible to overcome. This is how practicing meditation can be rewarding on its own, and give you motivation to continue, instead of being something that you feel obligated to do.

## Chapter 4: Why Should You Use Mindfulness?

Mindfulness and meditation, in general, are great for you. Why? Well, here are a number

of reasons.

☐ Mindfulness is a stressbuster. We experience negative effects of our modernized

lives. What we have are countless hours of stress piled upon stress, and almost no

breaks in between. Our minds and bodies are constantly over-clocked, and may even be so while asleep! Sometimes, a simple visit to the doctor can help. A few

lifestyle changes here and there, some sort of medication, plus some money to pay for the fees, and stress issues might be resolved - temporarily. Count a few weeks and we're back to saying and doing things we wish we hadn't.

But where do you think the best doctors turn to when their patients won't get better? Therapists, they're who - those who know and practice mindfulness and can teach them to others. People may be overwhelmed by work or family affairs, and some might be simply seeking for a way out of their boxed regimens.

Whatever the reason, mindfulness works against stress and its effects on the body.

And you don't even have to shell out money for it!

☐ You'll be able to focus on your senses. You use your senses in your everyday life,

but do you actually get to focus on them? Are you able to actually be thankful for them and understand their role in your life? Probably not, right? The key here is to spend just one day in your life trying to be aware of them so that you'll also know how to use them the best way you can.

☐ You'll be able to chesih non-verbal experiences. You get to somehow enjoy life

without trying to explain things too much. You get to understand that there is a vast world of difference between hearing and listening, or talking and speaking. You get to be a highly spiritual, rather than superficial person.

☐ You get to g through your feelings one at a time. Again, it's all about feeling

what you need to feel¼ no matter how good or awful they are.

☐ You'll be more content in life, but you'll also realize that you can keep on

dreaming and work on those dreams so they could come true.

☐ Mindfulness helps build relationships. You'll be able to relate to people more and

realize that everyone has the battle to fight. That's why you should just help each other out instead of bringing one another down.

☐ Some of the most stressful things in life are those that make it turn - the people.

Like it or not, we have to deal with them since our relationships can make or break a lot of things. That said, a person who practices mindfulness can help turn

even the worst of relationship woes into something better.

When the practice of mindfulness was transplanted to the West from its Oriental

origins, it seemed to lose a lot of things. Suddenly, the practice was all about self-improving oneself, presumably in order to put him above others. This might have been inevitable at first, but this way, it has lost much of its meaning.

Let's think of it this way - when you have problems, it is so easy to mull over it

and sulk. This is regardless of the magnitude of your concern. Mundane things

can be blown up to such a proportion that we lose sight of the bigger picture (case

in point: social media). However, when we are mindful of things such as our

problems, we begin to consider things in a more altruistic light. We see how this problem fits into the bigger picture of our surroundings and our relations. Thus, we are less likely to blow things up by taking out our frustrations on a colleague

or a loved one. And if the issue is with another person, we get to see things in

their eyes as well - an important step in avoiding conflict and healing wounded feelings.

In the end, mindfulness is as much a way to improve one's outlook on others inasmuch as it helps him improve himself.

☐ You'll be more motivated to work or be great at whatever it is that you're doing in

life.

☐ You'll be a happier individual. You'll feel less alone and you'll realize that you

don't have to fight your battles alone anymore.

☐ You get to recognize the emotions that you are feeling and you also get to name them in your mind. For example, after watching a really heartbreaking movie, you

start crying - this emotion is called sadness - or when you see a friend you have not seen in so long and you feel like your heart is bursting with happiness - well, you feel joy.

☐ You get to accept your emotions, but you do not let them take over your life.

Some people hate recognizing emotions. On being heartbroken, they go out, party,

drink,—without actually accepting the fact that they're sad and heartbroken, and

thus, the healing process takes a long time. When you accept your emotions, you'll notice how easier life can be.

☐ You get to become curious about your experiences, and so in turn, you get to

investigate them, while feeling different sensations within you.

☐ Mindfulness is realistic. When something is wearing us out, everyone will caution us to avoid it. So what if the thing that wears you down is your daily life?

Everyone will tell you to make changes - changes so substantial that they are

hardly realistic. Indeed, making such changes can be no different from dieting -

you try and try to stick to it, but there are times when you "just slip". And like

how weight gain comes faster after a failed diet, so does stress strike harder after you know you've failed your mission to change.

So what's the solution? Something realistic - something that can fit into the daily framework while also being solidly effective.

Mindfulness is your best bet - it is backed by science and thousands of years of effective practice. Once you understand its principles, you can easily integrate it

into your daily life. You should not live like a hermit to be a mindful person - you only need to understand the concepts behind it.

You see, these things will make you a better, stronger, and definitely happier person.

## Chapter 5: What Is Mindfulness?

Mindfulness is the practice and ability to sit in the present moment with awareness. This awareness is a calm state of mind that allows us to be with whatever is going on in our lives in a nonreactive way. It is a way to not judge our current situations and to observe objectively. Mindfulness is paying attention to the present moment.

When we practice mindfulness, our everyday stresses will not cause us to push the panic button when things don't seem to be going our way.

Benefits of Mindfulness

Awareness of self

Self-control

Stress relief

Lower blood pressure

Less chronic pain

Better sleep

Improved mental health

Enhanced focus and concentration

How to Practice Mindfulness

Mindfulness can be practiced through meditation. When done on a regular basis, it can bring much ease to daily life and calm other life stresses. This is what it means to live mindfully, but it does take practice outside of just daily life itself.

Ways to practice becoming mindful include noticing your feelings and thoughts without letting them affect you or noticing sensations in the body such as touch, sight or sound to witness your experience in the moment. It is a way to hone in on the here and now, to train our minds to be free of distraction, so we can let go of those old ways of being that do not serve us to be our best.

If you're wondering what you can do to break the stress bubble in your life, know that you have options. And they start with you, first and foremost!

Ways to Beat Stress and Practice Mindfulness

## Take a Deep Breath

"Breath is the king of mind."
— B.K.S. Iyengar, Light on Yoga

It may sound cliché, but this is a tried and true method to combat stress in the moment. Did you know that breathing is the biggest way our bodies detoxify itself? The act of breathing is your body's way of getting rid of wanted toxins and bringing in a fresh supply of oxygen to replenish the cells that need to continue working for you.

When you feel anxious thoughts running through your mind, stop wherever you are. Take a long, slow deep inhalation through your nose followed by an exhalation through your mouth. It could be slightly audible with a sound, like a sigh, to really help relieve tension. Take at least 3 of these deep, full breaths. You can do as many as you like. The beauty is that we are always breathing! When we connect to our breath, we bring ourselves into the present moment and away from our worries about the past or future.

Meditate

Meditation is a great tool to practice regularly to combat daily stressors. With a regular practice, one can respond more mindfully to challenges that life throws us. There are many forms of meditation one can practice, and you may want to try a few before sticking to just one.

A great meditation to begin with is mindfulness meditation. This type of meditation focuses on one aspect, such as the breath or another type of sensory experience, in order to draw the mind inward. This brings us out of our heads and into a quiet place. Even if the thoughts and worries do not stop immediately, it is okay. That is not necessarily the purpose. The purpose is that when those thoughts and worries come into our minds, we have something to bring ourselves back to- the focal point of the meditation.

For example, the focus of the meditation may be on counting the breath. Perhaps you count each inhale and exhale up to a count of 10, and then repeat again for 10 minutes. Whenever the mind becomes distracted, just start over. You will realize there is no need to get angry with yourself about it. And you may find, in turn, this practice will you help not overreact when you make mistakes in the future (because we all make them!)

Exercise

But a yogi never forgets that health must begin with the body. Your body is the child of the soul. You must nourish and train your child. Physical health is not a commodity to be bargained for. Nor can it be swallowed in the form of drugs and pills. It has to be earned through sweat."
— B.K.S. Iyengar

Exercise is one of the best ways to combat stress, and you'll get stronger while you're at it. It's a win-win situation. Exercise is proven to make us feel better by releasing feel-good endorphins in the brain. Choose a workout that you enjoy, whether it's weight lifting or running, or even just taking long walks, it doesn't matter.

Whatever it may be, your exercise routine will bring you into the action of your physical body and out of the happenings of your mind. Give your mind a break! If you sit all day at work, chances are your body doesn't get enough exercise and your mind gets too much. And if you're job is physically demanding, you may need a little extra cross-training to fight off wear and tear that can cause injury.

Laughter

Next time you feel stressed, laugh it out. You know the saying, "laughter is the best medicine"? That's because it really is.

Give yourself a good belly laugh and notice how it makes you feel. Feel better? Probably. Laughter is known to lower the stress hormone, cortisol. Put on your favorite comedy or grab your favorite comic book and let the laughter roll in. Even better, try laughter yoga!

**5. Yoga**

The combination of moving, breathing, and meditating is a recipe for success to soothe any troubled mind. Yoga, an ancient spiritual practice from India, means to yoke or unite. It is a science that seeks to transcend this reality through merging the body, mind, and spirit. Even if that is not your goal, the basic physical practice can improve your mental health.

The physical postures that yoga has popularized in the West were originally created to prepare the body for long periods of meditation. Many poses are thought to merely be stretching postures, but the truth is there is a lot more than stretching happening in the body. While they can, of course, improve flexibility, the combination of the posture with the breath allows the practitioner to drop into a mindful, present place.

Yoga is a great place to practice mindfulness because your practice can be like a test run for life, but on your mat instead. Say, for example, you are taking a vinyasa class and you happen to really dislike chaturanga, but you know you need to do them to strengthen your shoulders and back muscles. Instead of cursing your instructor the next time she cues it and silently dreading the action, just observe the way you feel, move through it and then move on. This is practicing mindfulness- not letting our thoughts get in the way of our actions in a negative way.

Benefits of Mindfulness and Meditation

Meditation has a profound effect on the body and mind. New research by Harvard proves that meditation positively impacts brain health to increase grey matter, the stuff that helps our memories and cognitive abilities. In addition to this, meditation is known to activate the parasympathetic nervous system, also known as the 'rest and digest' system.

Effects of the PSNS:

Decreases heart rate

Relaxes muscles

Pupils constricted

Increased digestion and elimination

The parasympathetic nervous system is important because it helps the body rest from the stress of the day through good sleeping habits and also helps the body recover from any injuries While we cannot control the automatic beating of our hearts the same way we can control the automation of our breath, we can learn to train our body's response to stress through developing mindfulness techniques that activate a calm response (i.e. parasympathetic) versus an adrenaline-fueled response (sympathetic).

Meditation and mindfulness are the #1 things you can do for yourself to overcome depression and anxiety. They can even help you to lose weight if that is something you are struggling with! When it comes to changing our health and creating better habits, we must first decide that is what we want. This starts with the mind!

When the mind is riddled with fears, worries, and anxiety, it is hard to move forward to make necessary changes.

Depression

Mindfulness is a beneficial method to improve symptoms of depression. Common symptoms include feelings of hopelessness, memory dysfunction, impaired thinking, and difficulty concentrating. This condition can impact every part of life, from work to school and life at home. It seems like a never-ending vicious cycle, where negative thinking just leads to more negative thoughts.

Many times, those who suffer from depression may not even realize their thinking patterns. Mindfulness practices help them to come into the present moment, where they can acknowledge those thoughts and habits. It brings them into a nonjudgmental space where they can learn to recognize those negative thoughts are not, in fact, their true reality.

People who practice mindfulness give less power to those thoughts that try and bring them down. This is one of the greatest lessons mindfulness can teach us.

Anxiety

Anxiety is a condition that affects over 40 million Americans. It causes racing thoughts, elevated heart rate, body flushing, and feelings of panic. Many people turn to a quick fix, such as medication, which has many unwanted side effects. For a solution with only positive side effects, mindfulness and meditation is the answer. Meditation over medication!

While behavioral therapy is also an option, many may not have the resources or schedule to accommodate these sessions. With mindfulness/meditation, all you need is yourself. You don't have to drive anywhere or go somewhere special. It can be done anywhere and you can do it on your own time.

Anxiety literally causes a portion of the brain- the amygdala- to grow larger. The amygdala controls our fears and responses, which is the center of our fight or flight response. This is a primitive response mechanism designed to protect evolving humans during hunting. When enlarged, the central nervous system does not get a break and is overworked.

Meditation, however, shrinks this portion of the brain and also increases grey matter in the brain, according to a Harvard study. This is essential for cognitive functioning and memory abilities. What this means is that meditation can rewire your brain to be less anxious and more present! No more thoughts spinning through the brain like an endless hamster wheel. That does not have to be your life.

Weight Loss

The issues of depression and anxiety are often linked to being overweight, overeating, and obesity. The first step is using mindfulness to ease the symptoms of these conditions. Once we can become more mindful in our lives, then we can make the right choices when it comes to our diet and lifestyle choices.

If you live a sedentary and depressed life, working a 9-5 and coming home to watch

TV, it is natural to feel depressed. The facts are out there- exercise is good for you- not just physically, but also mentally. Exercise releases endorphins in the brain, which elevate your mood and make you feel good. Meditation, instead of vapid television watching, can first and foremost make us aware of our habits. Once we become aware of them, then we can make the plans to change the ones that affect us negatively.

Weight loss is, of course, a two-way street. When someone suffers from afflictions like depression, eating becomes an indulgence to make us feel better. The choices we make may not always be mindful. Over time this adds up to unhealthiness and serious weight gain.

However, through this practice, we can become mindful of what we eat. Perhaps start with meal planning, or eliminating certain foods from your diet that you know are harmful. It may take some time to figure out what truly works for you, but keeping general nutrient needs in mind while cutting out the excess sugars and calories in combination with a steady workout routine that fits with your schedule is going to work best. You will feel better and don't have to go crazy to make it happen!

## Chapter 6: Consciously Choose Awareness

Now that you know what mindfulness is and how it can improve your life, it's time to find out how to implement this powerful technique. You won't be able to achieve mindfulness without putting some effort and discipline into it. Mindfulness doesn't come automatically, in other words. It is a conscious choice that only you can make.

Decide If Mindfulness Is Right for You in This Moment

You just read many reasons to choose mindfulness. The question you need to ask yourself is if you're ready to begin your mindfulness practice. Although there's no time like the present to start, you might feel hesitant to plunge in right now. If so, that's okay.

Remember that you need to exercise discernment in making decisions. You don't need to judge yourself harshly about the decisions you want to make. If you're not ready to make the commitment you need to make in order to be successful at it, just read more about it and learn all you can. When the time is right, you'll choose mindfulness without hesitation.

Make a Commitment to Be Mindful

After you make a decision to be mindful, you need to make a concrete commitment to practice it every day. What form that commitment takes is entirely up to you. You could tell friends and family members about your choice. You might write down your commitment in a journal. Whatever it takes to make a real and lasting commitment to your mindfulness practice, take that step now.

Set Aside Specific Times to Be Mindful

Time is precious, but it's also plentiful. You have 24 hours in a day to schedule that way you choose. Set some specific times to practice mindful awareness in the coming days and weeks. You can write these times down on a desk calendar. Or, you can set up notifications for these times on your smartphone.

Many people find that the most convenient and surest way to remember your mindfulness schedule is to set up notifications on software like Outlook or Google Calendar. This is especially helpful if you spend a lot of time on your computer. Then, when the notifications come up, don't tell yourself you'll do it later. Do it right now, in that moment.

Choose Activities to Engage in Mindfully

Going by a clock or scheduling software or apps is a good way to make sure you fit mindfulness into your schedule. Another way is to choose activities you do every day and practice mindfulness as you do them. You can be mindful as you eat or take a daily walk in the park. You can also do a mindfulness meditation when you are riding a bus or sitting alone in a restaurant. Think about the things you do each day when you can go deeper into awareness. Try to choose ordinary activities that you do on any given day.

And, remember that mindfulness involves a unique type of focus and concentration, so at least when you're first learning mindfulness, don't pick times that require you to concentrate on something urgent. Choose a time that you're doing something that doesn't require great attention. As you grow in your mindfulness, it's possible that you can do anything mindfully.

Plan to Attend Mindfulness Classes, Workshops and Retreats

You might find that a money commitment to mindfulness is more effective than anything you could write in a journal or say to someone else about your new practice. If so, sign up for a mindfulness class, workshop or retreat. You'll not only anchor your commitment in practical realities, but you'll also get to spend time learning from experts in mindfulness.

## Chapter 7: Improving Your Practice

It is very interesting studying awareness of the mind because it demonstrates the effects of fantasies and thoughts. If your mind is constantly full of bright happy thoughts, if in excess, it can also cause your mind to lack in being able to focus on one thing.

Learning how to gently change your temper of state of consciousness, will improve your overall well being. When you may feel dissatisfied instead introduce appreciation, or when you are feeling depressed introduce compassion, and goodwill when you are feeling angry.

Work towards being aware without using labels or words to express this. Learn to have quiet awareness and word-less awareness. Being able to let go of stressful states in the body and mind is an essential part of the four foundations. You may find it difficult to be kind to yourself, but this is an important step in helping to release the stress exclusive of you judging yourself. The mind can jump into fear, distress, and confusion, over and over again. These are signs that the mind is inexperienced and wild. Once you become more familiar with practising mindfulness your mind will not react in the same way.

Transforming Your Mind Using Meditation.

First you need to understand that you cannot force your mind to change but instead you must approach your mind in a friendly way showing it that you want to make a friendly connection with it. This you will do by learning how your mind truly works. Don't try and suppress thoughts in your mind or try and erase things from your mind but instead allow these thoughts to pass peacefully. But you must also have some control over your mind do not totally surrender yourself to it. Become friends with your mind by finding out what your mind truly loves. The conceptual mind loves to be kept busy doing and thinking about things. It loves to get stimulated by learning new things and gaining new knowledge. If your mind is getting into trouble then it is a mind that is not being kept busy. You can give your mind the job of meditation. This will be a great win for you and your mind as you will be happy to know you are in charge of your own mind and your mind will be happy being kept busy working through meditation. Your conceptual mind will no longer have you trapped but you will be free to make choices in your life that will bring you to finding peace and contentment in your life.

Develop Meditation.

By continuing to practice Mindfulness you will learn how your body and mind is interacting, and you will have a deeper understanding of the structure of life. This will help to lead you towards a more happy and healthy life. You will be able to abandon the stressful events in life such as fear, ignorance, and greed but instead being aware of them. You can plan to carry Mindfulness across and learn to apply it to your everyday activities beyond just using them during meditation practice. You will find Mindfulness to be a helpful tool that you can use in just about every circumstance you will come across. Picture your mind as a lovely lotus flower that its roots are in the mud it is now standing beautiful and free!

When you start with meditation you want to begin at a level that will be easy for you to adjust to and will feel comfortable for you. In the modern world meditation has become a popular way to help us in dealing with the stresses and anxiety that come with living in this fast paced world. There have been different types of meditation that have come from Buddhism, Christianity, and Hinduism that can be classified in five main categories: 1) Concentration 2) Reflective Meditation 3) Mindfulness Meditation 4) Heart-Centered Meditation and 5) Creative Meditation. You do not have to begin with the classic meditation pose sitting cross-legged on the floor but you can sit on a chair if this is more comfortable for you. The main thing to concentrate on is making sure that you are seated in a comfortable position that suits you.

## Chapter 8: Depression

Mindfulness and giving your attention to the present moment is also known to be helpful when it comes to improving the symptoms of depression. These symptoms include distorted thinking, forgetfulness as well as the inability to properly concentrate – all of which can significantly impair a person's life.

This particular issue can affect any person of any age and whilst there are medications sometimes prescribed for it, experts suggest that natural treatments are still the best options. Here are some simple mindfulness exercises to help you get started:

Pause, identify and respond.

Mindfulness practices of MBCT allowed people to be more intentionally aware of the present moment, which gave them space to pause before reacting automatically to others. Doing this allows you to first step back instead of becoming instantly distressed about a difficult situation or a comment you didn't quite like. It also helps you to become more emphatic and attuned to the other person's emotions and needs. When this happens, you begin to see things from this perspective, which allows you to properly decide the course of action to take. You may not have control over your thoughts, but you can choose how to react. So PAUSE, IDENTIFY and RESPOND.

It's ok to say "no".

Mindfulness can also instil a sense of assertiveness, in that people become more comfortable when it comes to saying NO. This, in turn, lightens the load of responsibility placed upon their shoulders. They can easily recognize when something would be too much for them to handle and acknowledging the fact that it is okay to say no. This is putting their own needs first before anyone else's without being uncomfortable or feeling guilty about it. Note that it is not unusual for people who have depression to say yes in order to avoid any judgment from the second party. Mindfulness gives them the self-confidence to say otherwise and to be more assertive when choosing activities to take on.

Becoming more present with others.

In being present for other people, you are able to provide more attention to the important relationships that you have and make them feel appreciated. In turn, you will also gain an appreciation for them and enable you to become more open. Studies show that spending time with people who make you happy can help increase your energy, dispel any feelings of negativity and allow you to better cope with difficult situations. Spend time with family and friends, try to avoid isolating yourself whenever you're having a hard time. You'll find that just being with these people can sometimes be enough to push the negative emotions away.

Being aware of the depressed mind.

This is considered to be one of the most essential exercises that people need to practice if they are to use mindfulness to help with depression. Now, when one is depressed, it is like wearing very dark sunglasses. The mind cannot see anything good or beautiful; hence, it continues to spiral down into a deeper sadness. This lack of mindfulness skews up one's point of view.

Recognizing this is the first step of introducing awareness into the situation. By acknowledging that it is the mind's doing, the person can begin taking steps to change things. They can label the bad thoughts and separate it from the good ones, slowly but surely. With everyday practice and frequently reminding themselves that they have power over this depressed state of mind, they will be able to shift into one that's more empowering and helpful.

Be aware of the thoughts that fuel your depression.

Thoughts can be very powerful things especially if left to run rampant. A single thought can turn into something overwhelming in a matter of a few hours. Whilst some people do have better control over this, the depressed mind often cannot handle even the smallest of difficulties. For example, a small mistake to a person without depression is something they can easily brush off. To someone who's depressed, it can trigger a lot of negative thinking which can lead to them spiraling into despair.

Mindfulness brings insight into this as well as neutrality. It gives the person an outsider's perspective and makes him question the bad thoughts. This puts a stop to the flood of negativity and brings in much needed clarity.

Leave unhelpful thoughts alone.

Mindfulness is not about stopping negative thinking. Trying to stop your mind from doing so will be difficult and in the end, mentally exhaust you instead of helping you. Mindfulness will teach you how to leave your thoughts alone and shift your focus onto something else.

For example, you got bad marks in a subject and it is making you feel very sad and frustrated. You may begin a cycle of negative thinking when this happens. Instead of dwelling on the thoughts, you can shift your attention towards something more fruitful. Study for another subject or maybe read for pleasure. It won't be easy at first, but repetition should help with that.

Knowing your triggers.

Awareness also means knowing and understanding what triggers your depression. Are there specific situations wherein it begins to occur? Feelings of being tired, being overwhelmed or loneliness are just a few of the more common ones. Some people have visual triggers. Perhaps, a photo of a person you miss, a memorable place or even a line in a book you're reading.

Knowing these things will enable you to avoid them or at the very least, minimize the interaction you have with it. There is nothing wrong with separating yourself from the source of your depression. The important thing here is to recognize them and figure out how you want to handle them in the future. Take things slowly as you cannot simply delete these triggers from your life. Slowly, you may find that your aversion towards it lessens as well.

Give the exercises a try, the only way to find out if they'll work for you is if you actually practice them. Remember, there's always room for change and you can tweak these exercises to fit your preferences.

## Chapter 9: Deeper Exercises

Once you have practiced eating the grape and the partial body scan, you can move onto other exercises in mindfulness. Start by practicing these regularly. In the next section, we'll discuss how to tackle specific areas of anxiety using them.

Standing Yoga:

1. Stand with your feet on the floor. Breathe in deeply and raise your arms outwards, until they are in line with your shoulders. Hold this position for a few moments, breathing slowly and gently. Feel how your arms stretch and how the muscles hold your arms up. Do they feel heavy? Light? Is there pain anywhere? Notice all the sensations you feel.

2. Raise your arms further until they are above your head. Mindfully breathe in and out and feel the stretch going through your entire body. Can you feel the air on your skin? How does your stomach feel? Your shoulders? Your neck?

3. Slowly bring your arms back down past your sides, and as you do, roll your head forward toward your chest. Allow yourself to bend forward to the floor until you have reached a place that is comfortable for you. Don't try to force the stretch. Feel the weight of your head. Feel the stretch in the back of your legs. Breathe in and out for a few moments, noticing how you feel.

4. Roll your body up to a standing position, taking care that your head is the last thing to raise. Feel your spin as you roll back up to standing. Feel the muscles in your back. Can you feel any sensations? Is there any tension there you hadn't noticed before?

Repeat this stretch 2-3 more times, taking note each time of the sensations in a non-judgmental way.

Walking Mindfulness:

Plan a walk somewhere that will be peaceful and calm to begin. Plan to walk for at least 10 minutes.

1. Choose a path and begin to walk. Try to notice the way your legs move. How does it feel? Are you warm? Cool? Where are your arms? Are they tense or swinging by your side? Breathe in deeply and release, taking care to notice the sensation of the air filling your lungs and leaving as you continue to walk.

2. Begin to pay attention to the things you see? Are there trees? A path? Other people? What sounds can you hear?

3. Keep paying attention in this way as you continue to walk. If you find yourself getting distracted, then gently bring your attention back to the present moment by focusing n your breath or on any sounds you can hear.

Breathing Into Anxiety.

For this exercise sitting comfortably on a chair or lying down in bed will be useful. This meditation can become intense, so take a break if needed. Don't try to force yourself to stay with any sensations that are overwhelming.

1. Begin to mindfully breathe. Take care to notice how your body feels as a whole.

2. Now begin to focus on places in your body where you feel the most tension or anxiety. As you begin, you may think that the stress is only located in your mind. However, when new thoughts arise, try to see if there are any corresponding sensations in your body.

3. When you have found an area of anxiety of tension then fully bring your awareness to this spot. Use the technique described in the partial body scan. Focus on how it feels. Is it painful? Tense? What sorts of sensations are there? Try to observe them in a non-judgemental way.

4. Now breathe in mindfully and focus your breath entirely on the place you are feeling the anxiety. Try to notice how it feels. Is it hot? Shaky. Cold? Tense? Try to be right inside the sensation as you breathe in and out.

5. You may find that the sensation becomes intense. If it becomes too

uncomfortable then don't try to force yourself. Allow your attention to drift away from that focus. If you can, try to stay with it in this way – as part of your whole body, rather than giving your focus entirely to it.

6. When you are ready, consciously let go of the sensation. Remember to be non-judgemental. The idea of this exercise is not to invoke pain or to try and make things intense. Rather it is to explore feelings that are already there, in the framework of allowing and acceptance.

A number of years ago, I found myself dealing with a great deal of stress because of work. My main symptom was tenseness in my back along the spine that resulted in sleepless nights and frequent trips to the emergency room for

Full Body Scan

This exercise is an expanded version of the partial body scan. You will need to allow at least 30 minutes for this. You can either sit in a comfortable chair, or lie down.

1. Begin by taking some slow mindful breaths. As you breathe in, notice the feeling of the air entering your lungs. On the out breath, notice how it feels as it leaves your lungs. Notice your stomach rising and falling.

2. Begin at your left foot and follow the instructions for the partial body scan.

3. When you are ready, let go of the focus on your left foot and gently move to your ankle and lower leg. Mindfully examine and accept all the sensations you feel there. After a few moments let go of this and continue to move your attention up your body, until you reach the top of your hip. Feel the whole of the left leg. Notice any tension, or any warmth of tingling sensations. If you feel your mind wandering, gently bring it back to where it was before.

4. Let go of the attention on your left leg and move onto the toes of your right foot.

5. Repeat the exercise until you have turned your attention to your entire right leg. Then mindfully let go of the attention and focus on your hips, your lower abdomen and your groin area.

6. Continue to move up the body, paying close attention to your stomach, your back, your chest and your shoulder area.

7. You may find pockets of tension and anxiety in your shoulders especially. If this happens, note the sensation and then allow it to pass freely. Let your muscles relax if they are tense.

8. When you have reached your head and paid mindful attention to the sensations there, try to feel your entire body as a whole. Notice how it feels and what sensations, thoughts and emotions arise. When you are ready, mindfully let go of these sensations and finish the exercise.

## Chapter 10: Healthy Mindfulness Attitudes

After reaching a certain level of maturity, many of you will realize that not a lot of things in life are under your control. Of course, you can work hard to be successful and wealthy, but in the end, accidents, recessions, and just plain bad luck can get in the way. In fact, striving for control of external factors in your life can only lead to greater stress and anxiety.

The truth is, there is little about the outside world that you can control. You can't control what people think, how the weather will turn out, or how your business will be received. The only thing you can truly control is your attitude towards everything–how you experience life changes with the attitudes that you carry with you.

The Importance of Attitude

You can choose to experience everything through pessimism and negativity, or see the brighter side of the world. By employing mindful attitudes and change how you experience life, you can live a more fulfilling and happier life.

Indeed, attitude has a huge effect on the outcome of your endeavors. If you go forward with a positive attitude, it is more likely that the outcome becomes positive as well. Just think of going to a party at your parent's house. If you go there already anticipating a dull, unsavory night, then it's more likely that you're going to walk away with.

However, if you head out to that party ready for a good time, with a desire to enjoy yourself and entertain your parent's guests, then there will surely be a lot of enjoyment to be had.

Also, having altogether positive and mindful attitude will keep you from getting stressed, even in stressful situations, while having negative attitudes can make you stressed even in non-stressful situations.

Attitude Affects your Practice

If you go into your mindfulness practice with discouraging thoughts, prejudices or preconceptions, then the experience will reflect them. If your attitude is: "I don't think this will work," then it most likely won't. If you think: "This is really easy, I'm sure I can perfect it in no time," the first bump in the road can discourage you and shake up your entire practice.

What's the best attitude to have if you plan to practice mindfulness meditation? An attitude of openness. Simply say "I'm not sure how it will go. I'll wait and see what happens." This way, you are prepared for whatever outcome. Remember that mindfulness is about the experience, and it should be what you should focus on.

Attitudes for Mindfulness

Attitudes are like habits. There are bad ones and good ones, and like habits, attitudes can also be changed for the better. There are helpful and non-helpful attitudes when it comes to mindfulness. To improve these attitudes, you need to figure out what your attitudes are towards meditation in general.

Once you understand your attitudes and where they originate, you can then work toward altering and improving them so that you can have attitudes that are conducive to a regular practice.

An easy way to delve into your own mind is to make a questionnaire. Start with what benefits you expect, what physical, mental and emotional changes you hope to notice. Then you can move on to what you think of meditation as a whole, and what words you associate with mindfulness. Be as honest as possible and write down as many answers as you can.

Afterwards, go through your answers. Are there any patterns? Are your answers more to the positive or the negative side? Do not be judgmental of your answers and just take them for what they are.

Developing "Good" Attitudes

Now that you have a clear idea of what your attitudes for mindfulness are, it is time to strengthen or alter them so that they can be conducive to your practice. These attitudes will strengthen your resolve and clarify your intention as you go through with your practice.

These attitudes are like seeds. If you water and care for them well with mindful attention, they will bear fruit and you will reap the harvest.

Acceptance - Acceptance is one of the best attitudes to have for mindfulness and is a basic foundation for a strong meditative practice. Acceptance simply means awareness of your experience without prejudices or biases. It is about allowing yourself to feel and be without any judgment, about being aware of the experience and the experience alone. For you to truly know yourself, you have to accept all aspects of you.

Of course, keep in mind that acceptance does not mean giving up. Accepting yourself and your faults does not mean being resigned to them. Acceptance, in this context, simply means accepting your experiences and reactions as they happen.

Acceptance can also be translated as acknowledgement. By acknowledging your emotions, and reactions, you are changing how you experience them and you can come to terms with your present situation. Through acceptance, you can take the first step towards transformation.

Patience. As mindfulness itself is a long-term practice, patience is an important attitude to have. Patience for yourself and things around you can help in your practice. If you think you are a rather impatient person, meditation is a great way to develop patience. Giving yourself time to sit quietly, accepting things as they happen, can help develop patience.

Patience is like a muscle that you can work on and train to make it stronger. Here are some things you can do to develop your patience:

When you are standing in line and find yourself becoming impatient, you can practice mindfulness by being aware of what goes on in your head rather than keeping an eye on the clock. Simply focus your awareness and be engulfed by the sensations and thoughts that fill your mind.You'll find the minutes flying by without any of the stress you usually feel.

When you are at the supermarket, go directly to the nearest queue rather than the shortest one. Simply be aware of your thoughts and emotions and practice some mindfulness.

When talking with someone, allow them to take control of the conversation. Listen more than speak and wait for them to fill the silence. As much as you can, do away with the need to speed up or take control of the conversation. Listening and waiting for their response is a great way to develop patience.

Cultivating a beginner's mind.A beginner's mind is needed if you really want to go far in your mindfulness meditation practice. Simply put, a beginner's mind is one that has no knowledge, preconceptions, biases, and prejudices. It is open and empty. The beginner's mind is open to new ideas and has room for new experiences and new points of view.

Having a beginner's mind is like having the mind of a child. Notice how everything is new and amazing to a child, how everything can be a delight to him, and how much happier he is. To be truly mindful, you must see the world with fresh eyes and an open heart. Children laugh, dance and sing without worrying about how people will see them, or if they look ridiculous. They do it because they are happy and that is how they feel.

It is the same with mindfulness meditation. As mentioned above, the best attitude you can have to cultivate a strong practice is a wait-and-see one. Try to go into your practice without expectations and preconceptions, welcome each thought and sensation with focused awareness. Don't judge your experience. Simply lose yourself in it with mindful attention.

Experiencingthe world through a beginner's mind opens you up to wonder, fascination, fun, curiosity and creativity. As you empty your mind of preconceived notions, you find yourself discovering everything over again, but with eyes filled with joy and wonder.

Curiosity. Curiosity breeds knowledge. It is only with curiosity that you will continue to learn throughout your life. Someone who is curious is someone who is fully connected to his senses, because to him, every new sight and sound is a potential for a new discovery.

Developing a sense of curiosity in your practice is important. Mindfulness can even develop automatically with a curious mind as you will tend to pay attention to little things so that you can figure things out.

In your meditative practice, try to be curious. Explore the boundaries of your mind and your practice and find answers to your questions about life. Be curious about the emotions and thoughts that pop up into your mind as you meditate. The more mindful you become, the more you will find out about yourself.

The ability to let go. Another big cause of stress for many people is their inability to let things go. This can translate to holding on to regrets, feelings of guilt or grudges. Whatever the reason, it is this inability to let go that causes a lot of anxiety and negative emotions in people.

There are things in life that cannot be controlled or changed, especially when it comes to things that have happened in the past. You need to let things go so that you can move on and continue to grow.

It is the same in meditation. When thoughts and emotions pop up in your head, you should accept and acknowledge them then let go. This is the essence of true mindfulness. You let go of the past and future so that you are ready to be aware and accept the present, from moment to moment.

Here is a simple exercise to help you let go of past regrets, guilt or grudges:

Visualize yourself riding a hot air balloon with different sized weight hanging from the balloon.

Imagine that the balloons are labeled with the things you are unable to let go. You can bring to mind a wrong someone did that you can't forget, or a mistake you made. Label the weights one by one. Notice if there are any physical reactions as you bring these experiences to mind. Note which parts of your body are reacting (ex: a tightness in the neck, a knot in the stomach etc.).

Visualize yourself cutting the rope and feeling the balloon rise, but only slightly. Now visualize yourself cutting off the knots that hold one of the weights, while at the same time, remembering the part of your body that tensed up when you recalled the incident that the weight represents. Note the feelings that arise as you cut the weight off of the balloon.

Visualize yourself rising as the weight is cut off. Continue to do this until you are amongst the clouds. Note how you feel.

Kindness and Compassion. Whatever you do always has a certain quality to it, for example, the act of speaking. You can speak with an air of coldness and disdain, or with warmth and kindness. The act itself, even the words, may be the same but the quality is different, and so is the experience. When you bring kindness and compassion into the act, the experience itself changes. It may be a neutral or even unpleasant experience, but with kindness and compassion, you can transform it into something more positive.

Mindfulness isn't just about focused attention, but focused attention with a sense of warmth. You are attentive to your own emotions, but your attention has warmth and compassion with it.

Try to be aware of any critical thoughts that you have for yourself, accept these thoughts and feelings, and gently transform with your compassion and kindness. With warmth, kindness and compassion, you can dramatically change how you experience things. Endeavors become easier when you do it with positive intentions.

Thankfulness. More often than not, people tend to focus on what's missing from life rather than what's already there. This is the reason behind the constant wants and desires that many people have. They believe that they will be happier with a bigger house, a nicer car, the newest phone model, or a higher paying job. However, you can't really buy happiness with things, promotions or achievements. Happiness is a state of being that you can reach with the proper attitude.

Thankfulness simply means being grateful for all the things that you already have. This happens when you become more aware of the things that you already have rather than the things that you don't. This means cherishing your relationships, achievements, and place in life as it is.

Thankfulness has even been shown to have a direct correlation with well-being as a whole. This is no surprise, as being thankful and cherishing what you already have means you can nurture better quality relationships and have positive daily activities.

The attitudes that you bring with you affect how you experience day to day acts. These positive, helpful attitudes will not only make mindfulness easier to practice; these can also make you a better and happier person. Remember that even though you cannot control life, you can control your attitude towards it. Turning everyday into a positive and happy experience is within your control.

## Chapter 11: How To Meditate

The purpose of meditation is to target and quiet your brain, eventually reaching an increased degree of awareness and inner calm. It could come as a shock to discover that you can meditate anywhere and anytime, allowing you to ultimately access a feeling of tranquility and serenity no matter what's happening around you.

Getting ready to Meditate

Select a peaceful environment. Meditation should be used someplace soothing and peaceful. This will allow you to target exclusively on the duty available and prevent bombarding your brain with outdoors stimuli. Look for a location where you won't be interrupted throughout your deep breathing - whether it continues 5 minutes or around 30 minutes. The space doesn't need to be large - a walk-in wardrobe or even your workplace can be utilized for meditation, so long as it's someplace private.

For those not used to meditation, it's especially important to avoid any exterior distractions. Switch off Television sets, the telephone or other noisy home appliances. In the event that you play music, choose relaxed, repetitive and mild tunes, in order never to break your focus. Another option is to carefully turn on a little drinking water fountain - the audio of running drinking water can be hugely calming.

Recognize that the deep breathing space doesn't need to be completely silent, so there must be you don't need to grab the earplugs. The sound of the lawnmower operating or your dog barking nearby shouldn't prevent effective meditation. In fact, being conscious of these sounds but not permitting them to dominate your ideas can be an important element of successful deep breathing.

Meditating outside works for most meditators. So long as you don't sit down near an occupied roadway or another way to obtain loud sound, you will get peacefulness under a tree or seated upon some lush lawn in a favorite part of your garden.

Wear comfortable clothes. Among the major goals of meditation is to relaxed your brain and filter exterior factors. This is difficult in the event that you feel actually uncomfortable credited to limited or restrictive clothing. Make an effort to wear loose clothing during meditation practice and be sure to remove your shoes.

Wear a sweater or cardigan if you intend on meditating someplace cool. Unless you, the feeling to be chilly will consume your ideas and you'll be enticed to slice your practice brief.

If you're at work, or someplace that you can't easily change your clothes, do your very best to make yourself as comfortable as you can. Remove your shoes and coat, open up the collar of your t-shirt or blouse and remove your belt.

Determine how long you want to meditate. Before starting, you should determine how long you will meditate. Even though many seasoned mediators recommend twenty minute classes double each day, beginners can begin out doing less than five minutes, once a full day.

It's also advisable to make an effort to meditate at exactly the same time every day - be it a quarter-hour first thing each day, or 5 minutes on your lunch time hour. Whatever time you select, make an effort to make deep breathing an unshakable part of your day to day routine.

Once you've made the decision on a period framework, try to stay with it. Don't just quit because you are feeling enjoy it isn't working - it will require time and practice to accomplish successful meditation - right now, the most crucial thing is to keep attempting.

Although you should keep an eye on your deep breathing time, it isn't good for be constantly looking at your watch. Think about establishing a gentle security alarm to alert you whenever your practice is up, or time your practice to get rid of with a certain event - such as your lover getting up, or sunlight striking.

Stretch out. Deep breathing involves sitting in a single place for a certain time frame, so that it is important to reduce any pressure or tightness before starting. Doing a short while of light extending can certainly help to release you up and prepare both the body and brain for meditation. It will also prevent you from focusing on any sore spots rather than relaxing your mind.

Be sure you extend your throat and shoulder blades, particularly if you've been near a pc, also keep in mind your back. Extending out your hip and legs, especially those on the internal thigh, are a good idea when meditating in the lotus position.

Sit down in a comfortable position. As mentioned above, it is vital that you will be comfortable when you meditate, which explains why locating the best position for you is vital. Traditionally, deep breathing is utilized by sitting on the cushion on the floor, in a lotus, or half-lotus position. Unless your hip and legs, hips, and low back again are very versatile, lotus postures have a tendency to bow your low back again and stop you from managing your torso around your backbone. Select a position which allows you to be well balanced high and directly.

However, you can also sit down without crossing your hip and legs, on a cushioning, chair, or meditation bench. Your pelvis must be tilted forwards enough for your backbone to be focused over both bony pieces in the sofa, the places that bear your bodyweight. To tilt your pelvis in to the right position, take a seat on the ahead edge of the thick pillow, or place something about three or four 4 ins (7.6 or 10.2 cm) solid under the trunk legs of the chair. Meditation benches are usually constructed with a tilted chair. If not, put something under it to tilt it forwards between a fifty percent in and an inches.

The main thing is that you will be comfortable, relaxed, as well as your torso is well balanced which means that your backbone supports all your weight from the waist up.

Tilt your pelvis ahead. Then, beginning with your bottom, build up the vertebrae in your backbone, in order that they are well balanced one together with another and support the complete weight of your torso, throat, and head. It needs practice to get the position which allows you to relax your entire torso almost completely, only minor effort being utilized to maintain balance. Once you feel stress, relax the certain area. If you cannot relax it without slumping, check the point of your position and seek to re-balance your torso so that area can relax.

The traditional hands placement involves relaxing the hands in your lap, palms upward facing, with your right hands together with your remaining. However, you can also just rest the hands on your legs or leave them dangling down with you - whichever you like.

Close your eye. Deep breathing can be carried out with the eye open up or shut, however as a beginner it might be best to first try meditating with your eyes closed. This will filter any external visible stimulation and stop you from becoming sidetracked as you concentrate on calming your brain.

Once you've grown familiar with meditation, you can test training with your eye open. This is helpful if you discover you are either drifting off to sleep or concentrating too much with your eye shut, or if you are experiencing troubling mental images (which happens to a little proportion of individuals).

When you retain your eyes open up, you'll need to keep them "smooth" - that is, not centered on anything specifically. However, you do not want to get into a trance-like condition either - the target is to feel calm but alert.

Meditation Practices

Follow your respiration. The standard and universal of most deep breathing techniques, breathing meditation is a superb spot to start your practice. Pick a spot above your navel and concentrate on that spot with your mind. Notice the increasing and falling of your stomach as you inhale-exhale. Don't make a conscious work to improve your deep breathing patterns, breathe normally just.

Try to concentrate on your respiration in support of your deep breathing. Don't believe about your respiration or pass any kind of judgment from it (e.g. that breathing was shorter than the last one), just try to know it and become alert to it.

Some mental images which can help you include: imagining a coin seated at that moment above your navel, increasing and falling with your breathing; imagining a buoy floating in the sea, bobbing along with the swell and lull of your deep breathing; or imagining a lotus blossom seated in your stomach, unfurling its petals with every consumption of breath.

Don't get worried if your brain begins to wander - you are a newbie and, like anything, becoming proficient at meditation calls for practice. Just try to refocus your brain on your respiration and make an effort to think of nothing at all else. Drown out the chatter and try to clear your brain

Feel the body from the within. Is it possible to feel the power field within you, especially in your legs and arms? Unless you feel it, it's fine. But think: How are we in a position to move various areas of the body? It is the energy field that moves inside our body. Concentrating your attention on that energy field can not only help you stay static in todays but will help you connect to your being and circulation of life in you?

Try walking deep breathing. Walking meditation is alternative form of meditation which involves watching the motion of your toes and becoming alert to your body's link with the earth. In the event that you plan on carrying out long, seated deep breathing sessions, it may be beneficial to break them up with some walking meditation.

Choose a silent location to apply your walking deep breathing, with as few interruptions as you possibly can. The area doesn't have to be very large; nevertheless, you can walk at least seven paces in a right line before having to change. Remove your shoes, when possible.

Keeping your mind up with your gaze aimed directly forward, as well as your hands clasped jointly before you. Take a sluggish, deliberate step with your right feet. Just forget about any feelings or emotions in the feet and make an effort to focus on the motion itself. After taking the first rung on the ladder, stop for an instant before taking another. Only one foot should be moving at any moment.

When you reach the finish of your walking route, stop completely, with your ft together. Then, pivot on the right feet and change. Continue walking in the contrary path, using the same sluggish, deliberate motions as before.

While training walking meditation, try to concentrate on the movement of the feet and nothing else, in the same way that you concentrate on the rising and falling of your breath during breathing meditation. Make an effort to clear your brain and become alert to the connection in the middle of your feet and the planet earth below.

# Chapter 12: Mindfulness Meditation And Health Benefits

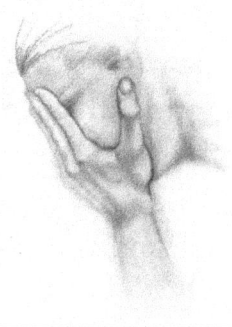

mindfulness meditation helps handle anxiety and depression

The two most common health problems faced by most people of today's busy world are depression and anxiety. The common cause to these issues is stress. For some people, stressful and disappointing incidences happening in their lives might just produce a short-lived symptom. But for others, the anxiety and depression caused can be ongoing and relentless, making their normal daily functioning impossible. Doctors and experts in the field agreed unanimously that mindfulness meditation is the best cure to anxiety and depression. Even those patients who are in advanced stages of depression can be recovered quickly with mindfulness meditation practices.

It's not easy to handle patients with anxiety and depression. It can be a long term challenge and even prove to be a vicious circle, wherein if the patients are not able to cope, they get more anxious in the cycle. Fortunately, we have the best cure to get out of this circle by adopting mindfulness meditation practices. It is an effortless and natural technique that can help end this self-perpetuating cycle.

Scientific researchers have shown that the deep relaxation and peace one gains from practicing mindfulness meditation settles the mind and the body, leading to a less stressed nervous system. Subsequently, disorders like depression and anxiety are decreased to a large extent. This enables you to overcome and manage most of the symptoms that might be experienced like that of attacks, panicky nature or possessing certain phobias etc. An analysis of all the published studies on anxiety and depression shows that mindfulness meditation is the best cure and is twice more effective than other techniques in curing these disorders.

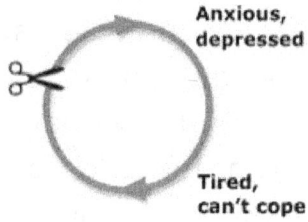

Mindfulness meditation

Recently, two studies examined more than 100 people in the age group of 55 years and older for the risk of cardiovascular disease. The result was that those people who were randomly assigned to practice mindfulness meditation showed an almost

47 percent decrease in symptoms of depression and other cardio diseases.

mindfulness meditation improves overall health

It is said that rest is the first prescription of doctor. By taking rest, the body heals naturally and functions to the fullest extent. If we don't take good rest, our body cannot function properly and it might be prone to issues relating to stress. Thus, rest is very important not only for the body but also for the mind. Both bodily rest and rest for the mind are conferred by mindfulness meditation.

Stress related problems are increasing day by day recently. More than 75% of the people who visit doctors complain about stress related issues. This is mainly because of the unending demand of the competitive atmosphere at work and at home. Those who deliver the most after stressing themselves mentally are the ones getting rewarded. Survival of the fittest is the motto in today's busy business world.

Moreover, stress affects each person differently. Some are not able to sleep well when they are under pressure at work; others might face digestive problems when stressed. Migraine, blood pressure, ulcers, asthma, cigarettes smoking, abuse of alcohol, other non-prescribed drug addiction, insomnia, depression, anxiety etc. are all known to be associated with stress. Moreover, the majority of these are issues that modern medical science is not effective in dealing with.

Fortunately, all these problems have been shown and proven to decrease with consistent practice of mindfulness meditation.

mindfulness meditation lowers blood pressure and diabetes

In a particular study conducted in a city, mindfulness meditation practices were compared with all the other widely practiced methods for providing people with mental relaxation. People who were suffering from high blood pressure and diabetes were told to follow mindfulness meditation. After few months, it was seen clearly that blood pressure dropped much more dramatically for those who were practicing mindfulness meditation than for those who adopted other techniques. Also, diabetes levels were seen to drop and maintain at right levels for mindfulness meditation practitioners.

mindfulness meditation cures addiction to alcohol, drugs and cigarette

Addiction to alcohol is the major cause of most of the anti-social problems today. People addicted to alcohol not only spoil their own health but also disturb the peace of mind of others around them, including their own family members. Besides shattering peace of mind, alcoholic addicts are major cause for most of the accidents that kill small children and adults on the roadside. Alcohol addiction is the worst addiction that brings about chaos and conflicts among neighbors and others. The worst part is that once people get addicted to alcohol, it is very difficult to recover to normal unless and until the addict cooperates. In most cases, even if the addict co-operates, the technique used for recovering might be so discouraging that it demands so much will power from that of the addict. Good news to the addicts' families is that mindfulness meditation has been proven to shows fantastic results with much strain on the part of the addict to control alcohol addiction. When mindfulness meditation helps in controlling the mind, it instills the will power and determination in the addicts to stop drinking since it is injurious not only for them but for people around them too.

mindfulness meditation supports women's health

Most women feel tired or frustrated or overwhelmed, or undergo short periods of depression or anxiety. This is mainly due to the fact that women play a vital and a most facetted role in our daily life. They have got to satisfy everyone's demand in the family and at the same time balance work life with personal household deeds too. Apart from time management, both mental and physical stress have been other challenges that women of today face. This kind of strain often leads to health problems that need to be taken care of then and there. The best method to have a check on women's health is to practice mindfulness meditation for both mental and physical stress management. Just a few minutes every day spent on mindfulness meditation can grant you with a peaceful time to switch off from all worldly functions and gain a profound state of mental and physical relief.

mindfulness meditation helps keep yourself young and energetic

Interestingly, most of the changes that took place in mindfulness meditation practitioners provided remedies against factors leading to ageing. This might not be a surprising result since mindfulness meditation is known to solve mental stress and depression caused due to even traumatic worries as well as simple day to day worries.

A controlled study on elderly people found that practicing mindfulness meditation lead to improvements in physical and mental health and general well-being.

Various researches show that people who practice mindfulness meditation possess the following:

- Increased level of creativity
- Increased life span
- Reduced biological age
- Higher levels of hormones that are responsible for juvenile and youthful look.
- Reduced requirements for health care

## mindfulness meditation helps children and teenagers

Mindfulness meditation practices provide special benefits for children and teenagers. By reducing stress and improving health, it helps children to concentrate better. By improving brain functioning and increasing focus and concentration, mindfulness meditation enhances better academic and other extracurricular activities results during school and college tenure. Also, meditation improves functioning of the right brain. This stimulates the genius qualities in the child and enhances fast brain development and intelligence.

Consistent practice of Mindfulness meditation provides children of all ages with the following benefits:

-More happiness with decreased chances of depression

-Less stress

-Ability to maintain calmer emotions and a sense of better control over themselves.

-Minimal exam tension and better concentration

-Highly enhanced levels of creativity and imagination

-Improved intelligence and brain functioning

-Better memory power and greater thirst to learn

-Higher levels of maturity, self-respect and self-confidence

-Good, restful sleep

-Improved overall health and general well-being

-Lesser temptation to smoke, to drink alcohol or to indulge in drugs.

## Chapter 13: Mindfulness? Yes Please!

Recent scientific findings have these benefits of practicing mindfulness.

University of New Mexico researchers found that participation in a Mindfulness exercise decreased anxiety and binge eating.

Office workers who practiced mindfulness for twenty minutes a day reported an average 11% reduction in perceived stress.

Eight weeks of mindfulness resulted in an improvement in the immune profiles of people with breast or prostate cancer, which corresponded with decreased depressive symptoms.

A prison offering mindfulness training for inmates found that those who completed the course showed lower levels of drug abuse, greater optimism, and better self-control, which could reduce recidivism.

Fifth-grade girls who did a ten-week program of mindfulness practices were more satisfied with their bodies and less preoccupied with weight.

A mix of cancer patients who tried mindfulness sessions showed significant improvement in mood and reduced stress. These results were maintained at a checkup six months later.

The likelihood of recurrence for patients who had experienced three or more bouts of depression was reduced by half through Mindfulness sessions.

After fifteen weeks of practicing mindfulness techniques, counseling students reported improved physical and emotional well-being, and a positive effect on their counseling skills and therapeutic relationships.

These research findings have affirm that daily mindfulness practice is good for your health. With that in mind, here are more reasons why you might want to consider incorporating mindfulness meditation into your daily life.

1. It lowers stress - really. Research published in Health Psychology shows that mindfulness is not only associated with **feeling** less stressed, it's also linked with decreased levels of the stress hormone cortisol.

2. It lets us learn about our true selves. Mindfulness can help us see beyond those colored glasses when we need to really analyze ourselves. A study in the journal Psychological Science shows that mindfulness can help us overcome common "blind spots," which can magnify or diminish our own flaws beyond reality.

3. It can make your grades better. Researchers from the University of California, Santa Barbara, found that college students who were trained in mindfulness performed better on the verbal reasoning section of the GRE, and also experienced improvements in their working memory.

4. It could help our troops. The U.S. Marine Corps are testing how mindfulness meditation training can improve troops'

performance and ability to handle -- and recover from -- stress.

5. It changes the brain in a protective way. University of Oregon researchers found that integrative body-mind training can actually result in brain changes that may be protective against mental illness.

6. It makes music sound better. Mindfulness meditation improves our focused enjoyment in music, helping us to truly enjoy to what we're listening to, according to a study in the journal Psychology of Music.

7. It helps us even when we're not actively practicing it. That's the finding of a study in the journal Frontiers in Human Neuroscience, which shows that the amygdala brain region's reaction to emotional stimuli is changed by meditation, and this effect occurs even when a person isn't actively meditating.

8. It makes you a better person. It could also benefit people we interact with, by making us more compassionate,

according to a study in the journal Psychological Science. Researchers from Northeastern and Harvard universities found that meditation is linked with more virtuous, "do-good" behavior.

9. It could help the elderly feel less lonely. Loneliness among seniors can be deadly, in that it's known to raise a number of health conditions. But researchers from the University of California, Los Angeles, found that mindfulness meditation helped to decrease these feelings of loneliness among the elderly, while at the same time boosting their health by reducing the expression of genes linked with inflammation.

10. It lowers depression risk among pregnant women. As many as one in five pregnant women will experience depression, but those who are at especially high risk for depression may benefit from some mindfulness session.

11. It lowers depression risk among growing teens. Teaching teens how

to practice mindfulness through school programs could help them experience less stress, anxiety and depression, according to a study from the University of Leuven.

12. It supports your weight-loss goals. Mindfulness could be your best friend, according to a survey of psychologists conducted by Consumer Reports and the American Psychological Association. Mindfulness training was considered an "excellent" approach for weight loss by seven out of 10 psychologists in the survey.

13. It helps you sleep better. I've saved the best for last! A University of Utah study found that mindfulness training not only help us better control our emotions and moods, but it can also help us sleep comfortably at night.

These reasons are enough to get you hooked with mindfulness training!

## Chapter 14: How Mindfulness Helps Ease Stress

Mindful living can help you fight and beat stress, no doubt. The question, however, is what really makes mindfulness so effective at combating stress?

**Mindfulness increases awareness of your thoughts:** Mindfulness helps you know the type of thoughts playing out in your mind. This way, you can step back from such thoughts and consider them critically instead of taking them literally. This ensures that your thoughts do not initiate the stress response.

**It helps delay your reaction to situations:** Instead of reacting promptly to situations without prior thoughts, mindfulness helps you pause for a moment, and then critically consider the situation at hand before you come up with the best way to tackle it.

**Mindfulness turns on your "being" mode and keeps your "doing" mode inactive:**

When you are mindful, you get used to being in a "being mode." The being mode is the mode associated with a state of relaxation while the "doing mode" is the mode associated with your action state. The action state initiates the stress response. Therefore, when you are in the being mode, you are relaxed, no action takes place and as such, the body does not trigger the stress response.

**Mindfulness increases awareness and sensitivity to your body's needs:** Mindfulness will help you take note of pains in your body, which will help you take necessary action to ensure these pains do not lead to increased stress in the body.

**It increases emotional intelligence:** Mindfulness helps you become more aware of the feelings and emotions of the people around you, and as your emotional intelligence increases, you are less likely to engage in any conflicts that will leave you stressed out.

**Reduces activity in the amygdala:** The Amygdala plays a major role in your stress responses. In fact, the amygdala is the part of the brain solely responsible for turning on your stress responses. Mindfulness reduces the level of activity happening in this part of your brain, which in turn leads to reduced stress responses.

**Increased focus:** Mindfulness helps you focus more on your current task. Increased focus helps you do more in less time, and the more tasks you accomplish successfully, the less likely you are to go into what psychologists refer to as "the stress zone" thanks to reduced stress responses.

**Helps change your attitude towards stress:** Mindfulness causes an attitudinal change where instead of focusing on the negative effects of stress, you concentrate on how the stress and increased pressure can help you make necessary changes in your life so you can start enjoying a better life.

Now that we have a better understanding of what mindfulness is as well as its various scientifically proven benefits, let us discuss the various ways through which you can make mindfulness an integral part of your everyday life.

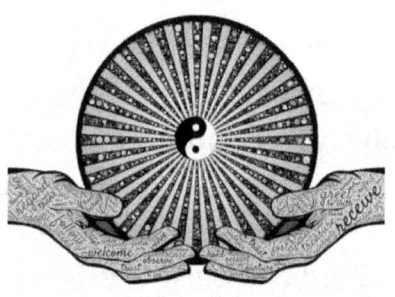

## Chapter 15: Meditation And Mindfulness

We all know that life can get very intense at times. Every day and in every moment we are overloaded with thoughts, concepts, people, things, perceptions, belief systems. Should I do this, should I do that? Money, relationships, assets, health, food, children – the list is endless. It is no wonder that we're all often so stressed, overloaded and confused. With all of this stimulation going on around us and inside of us in each moment, it's rather difficult to act from a space of awareness, clarity and peace.

Everything we do is driven by a belief system that is constructed by the knowledge we have accumulated and the perceptions we have based on past experiences. When we wake up in the morning and put on clothes, what we choose to wear is based on what is socially acceptable for a male or female to wear. Our choice also depends on what we'll be doing for the day. Will we just be chilling at home? Then comfortable clothes it is. If we have a meeting to attend today, formal clothing is what we will wear.

We are constantly processing, analyzing, imagining, thinking about the past or the future, and this shapes our experience of the present moment we are in. Most of our lives are lived in our minds.

If we come home from a long day at work, still frustrated by all the challenges and events that occurred, we are living in the past. We bring that frustration into the present moment, even though the challenges have long passed and we are no longer physically experiencing them.

This is an ironic situation we place ourselves in. We spend most of our day longing to be at home, but when we arrive at home, all we can think about is the day that just passed and the work we had to do. And let's not forget how much time we spend thinking about the next day – all the tasks, lists and challenges we'll have to face in the future. We do all of this instead of just simply being at home, in the moment and relief that our homes are supposed to bring us.

And so we live our lives somewhere else than where we actually are in the present moment, always waiting for the next moment to be happy or find peace.

Meditation as a tool for mindful living

Meditation is a tool used by millions of people around the world. Consistent practice of meditation allows you to sharpen your ability to focus on the present moment, thereby effortlessly unloading your mind from all the thoughts and stimulation that you process on a daily basis. Meditation alleviates the pressure and consumption of the past or the future – which are the places in your mind where we mostly experience stress or anxiety.

Every single moment we experience is one of a kind – it will never happen again or be experienced by anyone else in all of existence. It is an once-in-a-lifetime gift just for you. When you become truly present in the moment you are in, you come to realize the uniqueness, simplicity and beauty of each moment.

Let's try it out. Take a short moment to completely stop everything you are doing, and simply switch off your thoughts. Observe yourself and your surroundings – the beauty, perfection and natural aliveness of everything. Observe the gift of sight, of sound, the gift of your body and mind.

We encourage you to do this at least 10 times a day for 10 to 30 seconds. This will really help you come into the moment to witness the magic and blessings that surround you always. This daily practice will naturally shift your experience of life from one of worry, frustration and fear to one of empowerment, gratitude and centeredness.

If you feel the thoughts that generally cause stress or anxiety show up, know that this is normal. You have been giving these thoughts momentum your whole life – and just like a moving train, the more we press the breaks, the quicker it slows down. Your mind will gradually become better at focusing your attention where you prefer.

Because we spend the vast majority of life in our minds, we often miss the life that is happening right in front of us. We have conversations with people, but how often are

we truly listening? We walk past 4.5 billion years of evolution and beauty every day, but how often do we stop to acknowledge and appreciate it?

## Meditation techniques and styles

"Become the loving observer and gracious receiver of each new moment."

– Chloe Guilhermino

This definition of meditation may seem simple, but if you've tried the exercises above, you will find that having the ability to be focused on what is here and now seems impossible to achieve. And for the untrained mind, it probably is – unless you practice it over and over again.

Meditation is an art, so there are naturally many different variations to practice this age-old technique to create a centered and fulfilled life. But at the core of each of these techniques or styles is the goal to become present in each and every moment of your life.

Below is a short list of the different meditation techniques and styles. We encourage you to do own research, and to find the technique that suits you best as an individual (source: https://greatist.com/grow/science-backed-reasons-meditate ).

- Transcendental meditation
- Visualisation meditation
- Vipassana meditation
- Mantra meditation
- Guided meditation
- Yoga
- Qigong
- Breath or pranayama

Meditation teaches us how to bring our minds into our body and into our senses so that we can begin to experience life through our senses rather than through the perception of the mind. This is so that we may become aware of, and in tune with, the moment we are in. In this way, we are able really to taste the food we are eating, hear the person talking to us, feel what we are feeling, and see and appreciate all of who we are.

Through constant and focused practice, we will effortlessly become aware of the preciousness, beauty and gift that each moment holds. Your life will become a song unto itself as you savour and appreciate every moment and experience it for the perfection that it is. It is in this space that there can be no fear, stress or frustration.

The benefits of meditation

"Buddha was asked, 'What have you gained from meditation?' He replied, 'Nothing.' 'However,' Buddha said, 'let me tell you what I have lost: anger, anxiety, depression, insecurity, fear of old age and death'." – famous Buddha quote

There are a number of scientific benefits to regular meditation practice, including but not limited to:

- Reducing feelings of depression, anxiety, anger and confusion;
- Increasing blood flow and slowing the heart rate;
- Reducing pain and enhancing the body's immune system;
- Increasing energy; and
- Providing a sense of calm, peace and balance.

It is also said that people who meditate:

- Reduce their chance of having any sort of heart disease by 87%;
- Reduce the possibility of having cancer by 55%; and
- May look 12-15 years younger physiologically.  (source:

https://greatist.com/grow/science-backed-reasons-meditate )

As you go through your day, you collect various thought patterns, emotions and perceptions that play a huge role in how you see the world. Meditation allows us to unload the subconscious mind and deprogram ourselves from the conditioning and thought patterns that no longer serve us, so that we may align ourselves with a truer version of ourselves.

Meditation acts as a network between your true self, your mind and your body, allowing communication and awareness to take place between the three. By connecting your mind, body and soul, you deepen your understanding of your true self and also your life purpose. This knowledge will bring you a sense of peace, purpose and fulfillment.

Through constant daily practice, meditation will help you to develop a neutral mind. When your mind is neutral, you will act and react from a mind space that is free from judgement, perception or expectation. You will experience life, people or situations as

they truly are, liberating yourself from disappointment, frustration, anger, jealousy, sadness and irrelevant fears.

Additionally, meditation increases your intuition. This means you'll have a stronger sense of yourself, what is best for you, what is more aligned to your true self in any given moment. You will learn to trust yourself more and have absolute confidence in the decisions that you make – no matter how big or small they are.

As mediation is the process of also making the unconscious mind conscious, you will naturally let go of unconscious habits, fears and blocks, allowing you to move through life in a more fluid and harmonious way.

Meditation promotes the transformation of your emotions and mindset. The ability to focus your energy and thoughts to a place of your preference as well as enhancing overall effectiveness and efficiency is a great tool and asset to have.

In the stressful and fast-paced society we engage in on a daily basis, meditation puts the body and mind in a state of complete relaxation. This affords you the time to heal mentally and physically as you work through your thoughts and emotions. In this way, meditation is a similar process to sleeping, when we give ourselves the opportunity to reboot and recharge through relaxation.

Studies have also shown that meditation develops the frontal lobe of the brain, which governs our personality. So through daily practice, meditation can increase your self-awareness and allow you to feel free to express who you truly are.

Furthermore, meditation deepens your spiritual connection and understanding. By allowing yourself to become silent, you are able to connect to higher consciousness and experience a deep connection to all that is.

How to meditate

Meditation slowly, slowly turns into your enlightenment. You suddenly become aware one day, where is that darkness? Where is that continuous rush of thoughts? Where has the mind gone? Suddenly you are absolutely as hollow as a bamboo, but your hollowness is not empty – it is full of joy and full of rejoicing. You will dance for no reason at all, you will sing for no reason at all, songs that you have not composed, dances that you have not learned. They are just bubbling spontaneously in your consciousness. That is enlightenment, but don't make it a goal. Meditation is enough. Everything else follows on its own. – Osho

Absolutely anyone can meditate! And every individual's experience of meditation will be different, because it is a process of connecting with your true, unique self. And while sitting with crossed legs with your palms facing up might be the traditional setting we think of when it comes to meditation, there are a number of ways to connect with your true self, in a way that feels authentic to you and your experience.

Meditation can be engaging in anything that makes you feel alive, that brings you out of your mind and fully into the present moment. For some it is painting, singing, playing sports or even cooking. For others it is dancing, playing an instrument or practicing yoga.

All of these activities force you to be present and focused on the current moment, which is essentially what meditation is. And if what you practice is aligned with your true self, you will always feel happy and excited when practicing it. And afterwards it's almost assured that you will feel a sense of peace and purpose.

But for someone who does not know how to find their true passion or what excites them enough to take their focus away from the past and future, the easiest method of meditation is breath work.

Find a comfortable position and bring your mind into your body; focus on your breath. Instead of thinking about things, attune your mind to simply being in and experiencing the reality in front of you right now.

You will start to become aware of your physical body – the way it feels to be sitting, the sounds around you, the smells. Listen to your own heartbeat and just absorb everything around you, using all of your senses. Just observe – do not judge, do not analyze, do not

think. Stay in that moment for as long as you can, just observing the unfolding reality for what it is

This simple technique will open the doors to meditation for you, and the results will hopefully motivate you to include this practice in your daily life. And perhaps at a later stage, when you are more in tune with your true self, you will explore other methods of meditation that are more tailored to your true self.

## Meditation and affirmations

Using affirmations when meditating allows us to become conscious of our spoken words and the words we speak over our lives. If we say, 'I am always late', is it not so? If we say, 'I am always sick', is it not so? If we say, 'I am loving', is it not so? By saying certain affirmations or words over and over again on a daily basis, we begin to reprogram our minds, making space for us to shift ourselves into new belief systems, behaviours and experiences of ourselves and the world around us.

Let's do an exercise to set you on your path of using positive affirmations in your daily life. First, write down five things that you want to transform in yourself and your life. Make sure to use positive language and the present tense, as this greatly determines the effectiveness of your affirmations. For example: I am happy; I am healthy; I am beautiful; I am patient; I am love; I accept all that has happened in my life and so on.

We encourage you to personalize your affirmations. Let's say someone has wronged you in the past week and you feel upset about it. Your affirmation could be: I forgive this person; this person or situation no longer holds any power over me. And even if this is not the case and you have not forgiven this person or overcome the situation, your words have the power to alter that perception. Use your words to shift your perception of a situation and, sure enough, those words will become your reality. We are what we think – and we are also what we say. If you think or say you are unhappy, having a bad day, sick, lacking resources or whatever it may be, that is exactly what you will experience. It is important to already exist in the mindset we wish to be in and experience. And by writing down the affirmations, and then saying them out loud, you use both the written and spoken word to your advantage.

Using affirmations as a form of meditation is an incredibly powerful tool for self-transformation – it allows us to pinpoint certain aspects of our lives or ourselves and consciously shift them into a state of our preference.

It is clear that meditation is good for you, and every day more and more scientific studies are released on the benefits of this age-old practice. But how do you get started? How do you take the first step towards self-awareness and ultimately peace? Let's start with a few easy exercises:

Exercise 1:

The aim is to remain present for as long as possible.

First, let's start by setting a goal. Without following or buying into any thoughts or emotions or sensations that may arise, count three full breaths. Place all your focus and attention on your breath itself.

Thoughts may arise, and your mind may 'revolt' for a while at first – simply acknowledge it and know that this is part of the initial process. After a while, you may find that your ability to focus your mind solely on your breath will become better and better. This will bring with it a natural, pleasurable and beautiful sense of peace and renewal.

Continue to practice this short exercise several times a day until you feel satisfied with your performance. As time goes on and you feel more confident, you can increase your breath counts from three to six to twelve.

Repetition is key here, and constant practice will make it perfect. Soon you will be able to quieten your mind simply by taking a few breaths.

Exercise 2:

Take an aspect of your life that you would like to change. Write down a personal affirmation about this aspect, and remember to use positive, present language. Repeat this affirmation for two minutes, and then write about your experience of this. Do this exercise as often as possible until you see a shift in the situation or a change in your perception of it.

Here are a few examples of affirmations:

- In respect of finances: I am abundant; I am rich; I am prosperous; I am financially secure; I manage my finances well; money flows into my life effortlessly and abundantly.

- Your job: I am successful; I am good at what I do; I have a job that I love; I am the best I can be.

- Relationships: I love and accept this person; I forgive this person; balance and harmony fill this relationship; I am in a loving and kind relationship.

- Self: I am beautiful; I am happy; I accept and love myself; I am enough; I am healthy; I am worthy.

## Chapter 16: As A Man (Or Woman) Thinketh...

Meditation is key when we talk about changing our minds, redeeming it from an anxious, stressed or depressed state. Simply put, meditation is the act of training the mind or stimulating a particular type of consciousness in order to achieve particular benefits. These benefits include among others mental vitality, confidence and relaxation, all of which are the complete opposites of depression, anxiety and stress, respectively. Some of meditation's key benefits include:

More stable emotions;

Increased creativity;

Keener intuition;

Improved capacity to take care of challenges or problems; and

A consciousness-expanded mind that's sharper than ever.

Here are 3 good exercises for mindfulness meditation that can easily be done regardless of how busy our schedules become. These exercises can help us become more mindful of how we live our lives and win the fight versus anxiety, stress and even depression.

Taking Mindful Breaks

This particular exercise is especially useful and practical for those of us who are very busy with work. And it's pretty easy to do…simply take breaks – real breaks – from whatever it is we're doing. And by break, I mean both physical and mental breaks!

One of the best ways I do this is by using what's known as the Pomodoro Technique. It's a personal productivity method in which we work in 30-minute cycles. The first 25 minutes of each cycle is purely focused on work or the tasks at hand while the last 5 minutes are mandatory breaks or rests. On every 4th cycle, the 5-minute break or rest increases to 10 minutes before going back to the regular Pomodoro cycles of 25-5.

During the 5 or 10-minute breaks, I drop whatever it is I'm doing and sit comfortably with my eyes closed to notice or pay attention to how I'm mentally and physically feeling at the time. Then, I pay attention to the things I hear all around me such as the other room's ringing phone or the humming sound of the lights above. The key here is that I pay good attention to the things going on outside and inside me. Again, if random thoughts pop up – simply let them go and drift away.

Observation

In this exercise, just get any item that's well within your physical reach – any object will do. And while you hold your chosen object with your hands, just focus on said object intensely with your complete attention and allow yourself to be totally absorbed by it. If it's something you've already seen before, focus on or observe the object at a totally new (deeper?) level than you've ever had.

Keep in mind that as you focus on your chosen object, be careful not to exercise any judgment, evaluation or assessment of the object. Just focus on or be mindful of the object's visible attributes.

While doing this, notice a stronger sense of basking in the current moment, right here right now. As you consistently practice this, you'll find that your mind becomes better and better at quickly releasing past and future thoughts as well as experiencing the pleasurable sensations of simply being in the moment – right here and right now.

While this exercise looks very simple and subtle, don't underestimate its power. The methodology or the exercise itself may look "simple" but the changes you'll notice in your life as a result of consistently performing it can be very powerful.

Verbalizing Desires

The last mindfulness meditation exercise that you can do regularly to win the war against anxiety, stress and depression are positive affirmations, which are short statements about the things you desire to happen. These include the person you want to become, the goals you want to successfully achieve or the state you want to be in. These short statements are recited as often as possible with the expectation that these affirmations or statements can help condition the subconscious mind to become what is being repeatedly said. Good examples of such affirmations include:

In every way and in every day, I continue to become a better person inside and out.

I'm not a failure but am an overcomer and an achiever.

Failures aren't failures but opportunities to learn what really works.

Recite positive affirmations as often as possible for maximum effect. The more regularly it's done, the higher the chances and the faster such desires can come to pass. And by being mindful of one's desires, such desires become increasingly possible to achieve.

## Chapter 17: Mindfulness Exercises For Beginners

After sitting down, settling in, and cultivating the right attitudes towards meditation, it is now time to enter the state of mindfulness. This chapter discusses four exercises you can perform to achieve mindfulness meditation.

Mindful Breathing

You may wish to focus on mindfully counting your breaths at the moment. In this exercise, you do not think of the future anymore, nor think of the past. You do not think of your unfinished errands or past heartaches, because you are placing your full attention on the present moment, specifically on your breathing.

Start by taking three deep breaths. Breathe normally afterwards. Focus on the rims of your nostrils and let your breathing effortlessly flow in and out. Try to distinguish the parts of your breaths, including the brief pause in between finishing an inhalation and before beginning an exhalation. After exhalation, notice another brief pause before inhaling begins. The two pauses happen in such a brief moment that you are normally not aware of them. When you are mindful, however, you can fully appreciate them.

At the start of this exercise, you will have short inhalations and exhalations since your body and mind are not yet relaxed. Notice the feeling of that short inhalation and short exhalation as they occur. While doing this, your body and mind will eventually calm down and your breath lengthens and becomes subtle. Notice this peaceful and relaxing feeling of your breathing.

Concentration

In this exercise, you follow your in-breath from start to the end. Do this for your out-breath as well. If your in-breath is three or four seconds long, then your mindfulness will also be that long. Keep your focus on your breathing all throughout as air flows in and out of your body. In this way, mindfulness is uninterrupted and your awareness is sustained. This improves the quality of your concentration.

When you are breathing in, and then suddenly you remember, "Oh, I forgot to turn off the TV in the other room," then there is interruption in your concentration. Just stick to breathing all the way through so you become your in-breath and your out-breath. Continuing this will naturally make your breathing deeper, slower, more peaceful and harmonious.

Body Awareness

This exercise takes mindful breathing one step further. It is by becoming conscious of your entire body while you are breathing. "As I breathe in, I am conscious of my body. As I breathe out, I am conscious of my body." In the first exercise, you become conscious of your in-breath and out-breath. Since you now have created the energy of mindfulness by breathing, you can use that force to recognize your body and be fully aware that it is in this particular moment and space.

## Releasing Tension

This exercise releases accumulated tension, emotions, or pain in your body. When stresses build up inside you for a long time, the body suffers. The mind is not there to assist its release. Release tension by visiting each part of the body. Start, for example, with the right foot and work up to towards the top of your head. The aim is simply to be aware of whatever sensations (e.g. temperature, touch of clothing, pulse, current of energy, etc.) you are experiencing at every part of your body. Any relaxation that may be felt should be considered as just a by-product. Paradoxically, the more you consider mindfulness as a pure awareness exercise—without thinking or hoping for benefits—the more you improve your well-being.

## Chapter 18: Techniques Of Transcendental Meditation

The most useful approach to the practice of Transcendental Meditation is to consider it the most important activity of each day, planning it as if it were an appointment that cannot be missed. The ideal choice is early in the morning, before starting the day's activities. If this is not possible, it is a good rule to choose the best time for your own life and continue regularly. Some find it beneficial to practice twice a day: early in the morning after a restful sleep and in the late afternoon or early evening. However, a dedicated practice is recommended at least once a day.

Finding a place to Meditate

First you need to find a really peaceful place, that is free from intrusions and interruptions by others.

Aspirants to meditation often talk about obstacles created by family and friends. In most cases the fault lies in the aspirant. We talk too much. The way we use those fifteen minutes every morning is only about us, and there is no need to talk about it in the family, or to expect others to be quiet because we want to meditate. If we can't find a time for morning meditation because of family commitments, let's try to find some time later. There is always a way to overcome difficulties, when we are truly committed, a way that does not compromise our decision. As a last resort it is always possible to get up fifteen minutes earlier in the morning.

Position

Once the problem of time and place has been resolved, let's sit comfortably and begin to meditate. Here the question arises: how should we sit? Is the best position crossed-legged, kneeling, sitting, or standing? The best is always the simplest and most natural.

The cross-legged position was, and still is, widely used in the East, and many books have been written on this subject. Some of these positions are connected with the nervous system and with the inner structure of those subtle channels which the Hindus call "nadis", which are subjected to the nervous system recognized in the West.

The negative side of these positions is that they induce two rather undesirable reactions. In the first place they push us to concentrate on the mechanism and not on the purpose of the process and, secondly, they instigate us to frequently try a pleasant sense of superiority, based on the attempt to do something that the majority of people does not and that distinguishes us. In short, we are interested in the formal side of meditation; it deals with the non-self rather than the Self.

We therefore choose the position that most easily allows us to forget the physical body. For Westerners it is probably sitting. It is essential to keep the spine erect; stay relaxed (but not abandoned), so that no part of the body is in a state of tension, with the chin slightly reclined forward, so as to eliminate any stiffness in the back of the neck. Meditation is an inner act, and can only be performed successfully if the body is relaxed, in a balanced position and therefore forgotten.

Breathing

Once obtained a comfortable and relaxed position, and after having diverted the consciousness from the physical body, we turn our attention to the breath, to make sure that it is calm, regular and rhythmic.

At this point, I would like to warn against the use of breathing exercises, unless you have already devoted years to proper meditation and purification of the body. In ancient Eastern teachings, breath control was allowed only after the first three "means of union" (as they are called) were to some extent become part of life, and only by following appropriate instructions.

The practice of breathing exercises has nothing to do with spiritual development. This practice, which is instead connected with psychic development, creates many difficulties and is dangerous. In ancient times, the instructors carefully selected the subjects for this teaching and it was added as a complement to a formation that had already reached a certain degree of contact with the soul, so that it could direct the energies evoked by the breath towards its objectives.

We will therefore limit ourselves to ascertaining that the breath is calm and regular and we will completely withdraw the thoughts from the body to begin concentration.

Visualization and Creative use of Imagination

The next step in the practice of Transcendental Meditation is the use of imagination; we represent the triple lower man aligned or in direct communication with the soul. It is possible to do it in many ways. This is what is called visualization. One could say that visualization, imagination and will are the three most important factors in any creative process.

They are the subjective causes of many objective effects.

At the beginning, visualization is above all a matter of experimental faith. We know that, through reasoning, we have come to understand that within and beyond all manifested things there exists an Ideal Model that seeks to manifest itself on the physical plane. The use of visualization, imagination and will is part of the activities planned to accelerate the emergence of that Ideal.

When we visualize we use our highest conception of that ideal, covered with some kind of matter, usually mental, not yet being able to conceive higher forms or types of substance with which to wrap our images.

When we form a mental image, the substance of our mind vibrates at a certain frequency and attracts a corresponding type of mental substance in which the mind is immersed. Will keeps the image still and gives it life. This process takes place whether or not we are able to see it in the mind's eye. If we do not see it, it does not matter, as the creative work proceeds equally. Perhaps one day we will learn how to follow and consciously implement the whole process.

With regard to this work, sometimes in the initial phase the beginner represents the three bodies (the three aspects of formal nature) connected by a shining body of light, or visualizes three centers of vibrating energy, stimulated by a higher and more powerful center; others imagine the soul as a triangle of strength, to which the triangle of lower nature is connected by the silver thread that the Bible talks about, the sutratma, or thread of the soul of the Eastern Scriptures, or the life line of others schools of thought. Still others prefer to stick to the concept of a unified personality, connected to the immanent Divinity: the Christ in us, hope of glory.

The choice of the image to be used has little importance, as long as we start from the basic idea of the Self that seeks contact with the not-self, its instrument in the worlds of human expression and, vice versa, from the concept of non-self pushed to turn to its source of life. Once this is achieved, we can continue the meditation. The physical and emotional bodies fall, in turn, below the threshold of consciousness, we concentrate in the mind and try to bend it to our will.

From what we have said so far, the need for a Master is quite evident, that is a guide who knows how to accompany us to move correctly the first steps towards the practice of Transcendental Meditation.

Concentration

It is precisely at this point that our problem arises. The mind refuses to adhere to the thoughts we want to formulate and struggles in all directions in its usual search for subjects. We cannot concentrate on the thought itself and we think instead about what we will do later, about someone we have to talk to, or about a project that is close to our heart;

we begin to think of a person we love and immediately fall back into the world of emotions and we have to start all over again.

Then we gather our thoughts and start again with good success for half a minute, then we remember a commitment that we have taken or a job that we have to do and we find ourselves again in the field of mental reactions forgetting the line of thought we intended to follow. Once again we gather our scattered ideas and resume the work of taming the rebellious mind. Only with constant practice we will finally be able to maintain mental concentration with a certain degree of effectiveness.

How to reach this condition? Following a formula or a pattern of meditation that automatically establishes an insurmountable limit to the mind and tells it: "you can go there and no further". Carefully and thoughtfully we establish precise boundaries to mental activity, so that it is possible to see immediately when we cross them. We then know that we must withdraw ourselves again within the shelters that we ourselves have built.

The sincere investigator will try to start a form of meditation to help develop concentration.

In conclusion, these are the Stages of Transcendental Meditation:

1) Take a comfortable position that allows you to control your body.

2) Make sure the breath is rhythmic and regular.

3) Visualize the triple lower self (physical, emotional and mental): a) in contact with the soul; b) as a channel for soul energy directed to the brain through the mind. Now the physical apparatus can be controlled by the soul.

4) Focus precisely by appealing to the will. This means striving to keep the mind fixed on certain words, so that their meaning is clear in our mind and not just the words

themselves, or the fact that we are trying to meditate.

5)Repeat your Mantra with concentrated attention. An example of Mantra is: "More radiant than the sun, purer than snow, more subtler than ether is the Self, the Spirit that is in me. I am that Self. That Self is me."

6)Do not allow the mind to relax its concentration on the meaning, content or implications of the repeated Mantra.

7)Conclude intentionally the concentration work.

This is certainly a meditation for beginners. It contains some important points through which a thought gathering process is carried out and a refocusing method is used.

## Chapter 19: Practising Body Scan

You are now in the second day of this 7 days' mindfulness journey for self-discovery and enhancing own self-confidence ultimately; today, you will be doing physical body scanning meditation. We have already established that the process of engaging in mindful breathing which is regarded as breathing meditation during the first day of the mindfulness journey. In breathing meditation, you observe what goes on around and within you not with the intention to alter anything but to gain understanding and discover yourself through simply observing your own breathing. We able to use our breathing as a means of relieve from stress and anxiety.

Now you will be working on your body to become aware of it. This session will take approximately 6 minutes. If possible, make effort to continue the exercise beyond the first week in order to get amazing results. A 7 days' Mindfulness practice is a good start towards the result you desire but you can achieve more when you continue the practice. Mindfulness is the art of living in the moment; it is an enjoyable life journey. So, if you are dealing with stress and desire to enhance your confidence which is essential for success in any domains or industries, then you may consider to make Mindfulness your way of life.

$2^{nd}$ days' practice is a body scan exercise, it is simply taking notice of any sensation in your physical body at this present moment. Your present thought will affect your body. Be mindful that body scan practice may not be relaxing but you will relax eventually. Just feel, let it be and relax.

Notice your body

Do you notice how you respond to certain feeling especially emotional pain? Have you ever been in an uncomfortable situation before? The normal reaction we have for such feelings is to avoid, escape or to get rid of the pain or discomfort. But have you ever thought of accepting the pain or discomfort? The truth is that, pain and any other kind of undesirable feelings can be accepted and used to your advantage; this may sound impossible but it will be when you stop judging it and let it take its course like a river flow through the place where the pain is, be still and watch it goes by. Soon, you will find it no more.

In the animals' world, when an animal gets hurt, it will find a quiet place and be still and rest; human being somehow forgotten the feeling of being still and rest, thus feel your breathing, learn to feel the presence of your body and pay attention to any feelings and sensation of various parts of your body such as feet, hands, face, thighs, arm, shoulder, and even your muscles.

Here, we start the body scan practice:

$2^{nd}$ Day's Practice

Begin by bringing your attention to your body.

You may close your eyes, if it is more comfortable for you.

You may notice your body weight on the chair or on where you are seated.

Take a deep breath. Breathe-in slowly and breathe-out slowly.

Take another deep breath. Feel the air in and out of your nose.

Continue to take a few deep breaths.

As you inhale, you are bringing all the goodness to the body.

As you exhale, you are breathing out all toxic and unwanted stuffs out of your body.

You will soon have a sense of relaxation in your body and it continue to grow.

You may notice your feet on the floor and notice the sensations of your feet touching the floor.

Notice your weight on the chair.

Notice the clothe that touches your skin. Take your time.

Notice the sensation around your stomach, your chest, your shoulder, your hands, your neck, your mouth, your nose, your ear and your forehead.

Notice if any discomforts come with the sensation.

Acknowledge the discomfort, saying: "This is how I feel", if there is any.

Relax your body and allow it to go soften.

Notice the rising and falling of your chest and your stomach.

Soften your jaw. Allow your face and facial muscles to be soft.

Notice your body in the room you are in. Sense your own presence.

Take one deep breath, inhale 4-3-2-1, exhale 6-5-4-3-2-1.

Take another deep breath, inhale 4-3-2-1 and exhale 6-5-4-3-2-1.

When you are ready, you can open your eyes and notice you are back in the room.

INTERACTING WITH EXTERNAL WORLD

Today we will learn on how to interact with the external world mindfully. The exercise is simple and can be completed in a few minutes. Feel free to continue with the practice in your own comfortable way and stop whenever you want.

Every working adult knows what it takes to be professional in one's job. The price to pay may be managing tonnes of stress and sacrificing personal time with family and friends. The work demands in the modern world, in our society, are weighing heavily on our shoulders. How to live in peace with the world outside? We do not need to know how, we just need to let go and breathe. Your body knows how to inhale and it knows how to exhale; you need to exhale at time.

Most of the time we are so caught up with the demands of work that we hardly notice what are going on around us. A mindfulness practice on interacting with external world will help you to gain more awareness of your immediate environment which in turn will make you more flexible as you adapt to different working conditions in the office.

# 3rd Day's Practice

We will be doing the following exercises to sharper our awareness of the surrounding by noticing what is around us. Take your time to go through them one by one. So, if you are ready, let's start:

Sight: Look around you and name the 1st object as you look for 5 different objects, then do the same for the 2nd object out of those 5 objects, then the 3rd object out of those 5 objects and so on (example: blue book, red shirt, white watch, green leave, purple cup).

Sight & Touch: Look, name and touch 5 different objects, noticing their texture, temperature, mass and weight as you do so. Similarly, start with the 1st object, then do the same for the 2nd object, the 3rd object, the 4th object and lastly the 5th object.

Sight, Touch and Smell/Taste: Look at (things around you), name, taste and smell 5 different objects, noticing their colours, texture, taste and aroma. Start with the 1st object, then do the same for $2^{nd}$ object, $3^{rd}$ object till you complete the practice for all 5 objects.

Hearing: Close your eyes and listen for 5 different sounds. Count 5-4-3-2-1.

Take time and do the above exercise for two rounds. Practise breathing technique after each exercise: breathe-in count (silently) 4-3-2-1, hold breath count (silently) 2-1, breathe-out count (silently) 4-3-2-1. You are ready for your next challenge.

## Chapter 20: Mindfulness Techniques

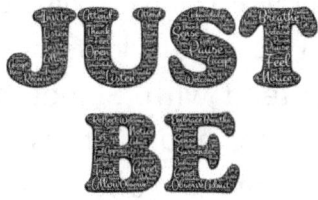

We've already discussed that mindfulness has far-reaching benefits to all who practice regularly but that benefits in general may not be sufficient to inspire students. As such, it's important to choose techniques which are most likely to be relative to those attending your class. The idea in the first instance is always to bring the concept of mindfulness to them and to then build upon these early foundations inspiring them in the process.

In this section, there are a series of tasks which can help bring awareness to the techniques and to introduce the principles

of each technique.
Creating space

The teenage years can be filled with angst – from worrying about their grades, to friendship fallouts, to bullying or even problems at home, students certainly have a lot to contend with. Sometimes (in the same way as for adults) it can be difficult to gain clarity of mind and so this is a great technique to allow students to gain space in their thoughts.

This is a very useful technique to help slow down a racing mind and it's easy to remember:

Use the acronym S.T.O.P.

S: Stop what you are doing

T: Take a breath –breathe in and out naturally. Use dialogue to coach yourself to breathing in and out to aid concentration.

O: Observe. Reflect on your thoughts and feelings. Consider your emotions too. Observe any damaging or negative thoughts where you may feel inadequate.

Mentally name your thoughts and notice how this calms.

P: Proceed. Support yourself in the moment.

Have the students write this down and talk about how and why it could help an emotive situation.

Task:

Another acronym based mindfulness task is R.A.I.N.

This helps to counteract difficult emotions.

R: Recognise strong emotions as they occur.

A: Acknowledge and allow the emotion.

I: Investigate – bringing self- analysis to the moment.

N: Non-identify– this serves to deflate and to minimise or to increase understanding that the emotion does not make up you the person, but represents a moment in time and a situation.

Teenagers are likely to have strong emotions – some will try to hide or refute these feelings, while acceptance and identifying an emotion helps the individual to view it from a safer distance recognizing that it is transient.

Task:

Teach the benefits of mindful walking. Consider it a meditation in movement.

Advise students that they must bring their attention to the sensations experienced in the feet and legs as they walk. Ensure the heel is placed first, then the ball of the foot, then the toes and then experience the movement. Connect with the motion, slow the pace, open up awareness, they should be in tune with their body. Now, they should turn their attention to their surroundings, connect with their senses, what do they see, hear, smell or feel?

They should consider the breeze against their skin, any dampness in the air, the warmth of the sun etc. Consider how much more in tune they will become with their surroundings as they walk.

Students can slip into a mindful state at any time they choose. They should learn to embrace the present and appreciating all the experiences as they happen.

Non-Judgemental Attitude

In life we are often judgemental, not just to ourselves but in respect of others. In mindfulness, we take an emotionally non-reactive state and so on a personal level, we do not judge whetherany experience is either good or bad. Where judgements are made, it's important to just notice them (extending awareness) and then to let go of them. Rather than being upset by the experience or, even a lack of it, it's important to accept it as is. Observe the experience in a mindful manner until it ceases to exist.

Pleasant or unpleasant experiences are treated in the same way.

Of course in a cognitive fashion, a mindful approach indicates whether an experience is good or bad but it is the emotional aspect in which we learn to not react, promoting stillness and balance of mind instead.

When we accept and experience an event, emotion or thought and refrain from pushing it away or the opposite, clinging to it or letting it overwhelm, we learn acceptance. When emotions are volatile, it's very difficult to accept or control an automatic reaction and this is where mindfulness comes in asit strengthens the individual's response and ability to simply be.

When you look at your students, many will respond to a situation in an emotive and potentially negative way. What we call the learning process i.e. how to react to certain situations, can become a potentially dangerous pattern of behaviour that is repeated. Mindfulness can help halt the creation of such patterns or help the individual to break the pattern in a conscious manner.

When emotions are strong or unpleasant we often find it difficult to accept the feeling. After all, it's not pleasant. As a result, many people start to feel bad about the experience and then develop concerns over feeling this way towards the experience. This just forms a vicious cycle that is not helpful and is fueled by negative thoughts.

Acceptance is a way of acknowledging all that the student is feeling and how much better is it if the student can learn to stand back from it so that the experiences are gained but so they are not defined by it. When you explain this to your students, you can help them identify the emotion, to accept but to locate the feeling which may be stored or experienced somewhere in the body.

Task:

Ask your students to consider a difficult experience, one which was emotive and even overwhelming. The situation may have left them feeling bad about the experience or about how they handled it. Ask them to recall the experience and then to consider:

☐ To try to shake the feeling
☐ To specify where in the body, the feeling may have been located
☐ To determine the colour or texture of the emotion
☐ To clarify whether anything changed

Although some students will find this whole process a little odd or even daunting, there's no doubt that this is an engaging task.

It is also a very important one because by locating the emotion we can determine that it is far smaller than we may first imagine. Alternatively, students are able to see that they are bigger than the whole emotion experienced so by standing back from the emotion as it occurs, they are not coloured by it. This is an excellent way of being able to avoid being caught up in the strength of the emotion and to apply a little space between them and the emotion itself.

When we embark upon the mindful approach, we refrain from becoming annoyed at being embroiled within the thoughts or, the emotions and instead learn to acknowledge its presence, letting it go without judgement and therefore, the focus is retained in the present moment.

## Chapter 21: Creativity

However busy your life is, try to leave room for the child inside you to come out from time to time. Whether this means sitting out on the lawn on a sunny day and blowing bubbles or taking off your shoes and socks and paddling in a brook, let yourself enjoy moments that you used to enjoy as a child. Be close up and personal with nature. You will find that you can build on your creative passions by doing this. You may, for example, notice the color of a pebble on a beach while it is wet and notice that the magical color seems to disappear when you move it out of water and it becomes dry. That's what happens to your viewpoint of life as well when you take no time to let the inner child out sometimes.

Whether you consider yourself creative or not, it's vital to your well-being that you enjoy some form of creativity. Bake a cake for someone who lives alone or make your own Christmas greetings cards from elements of nature that you found while walking in the woods. Whatever you choose to do, you need to create some form of balance in your life so that you have a fair share of each and every season that your life offers you. Enjoy the flowers of spring, by celebrating the warmer sunny days and walking outside after a long winter.

Remember when you look out of the window in the morning to be joyful and to contemplate on all of the things that make you feel grateful for life as these are all part and parcel of what's happening to you and how you feel. When you take this time alone and develop who you are, you become much more approachable to others. Your positivity shines and you are indeed whole. What too many people fret over in this day and age is being part of something – rather than being happy with simply being. People jump into relationships before having established a relationship with themselves. By using this alone time or this alone season to develop who you are, you open up the world to possibilities you may never have thought of before.

Doctors are so convinced about the benefits of mindfulness that they are now prescribing this for people who find themselves to be depressed or who feel isolated in the world because it reminds them that they are not really alone and that there is no need at all to feel isolated. When you can celebrate this time of being alone, you can use it to become a better person than you already are and learn to use the silences in your life to develop the spiritual side of your nature and your own self-realization.

During the course of reading this book, you will have seen that I have suggested different exercises and this is for a specific reason. YOU need to discover you. You are bombarded with all kinds of noise all through your life. The TV, the world in general and society expectations put all kinds of restrictions into our lives or make us feel bad about who we are. Silence allows you to assess who you are and work on the areas of your life that you feel are lacking. Creativity is one area that you may have neglected for a long time and you can choose to be creative in all different walks of life. To one person, that creativity may be in creating a garment. To another, it may be in enjoying washing the car and polishing it and seeing how the car shines in the sunlight. Your creativity is an individual thing.

Instead of feeling alone, feel privileged. Many people these days don't get alone time and want it. Use it to become the best version of yourself that you can be and celebrate it by using the freedom that it allows you to make the most of each season of your life. You will find that your positivity will shine and that the best version of you will attract the best versions of others.

You don't need other people to be the best person you can be. No lives are so intertwined that they need others to determine their value. In fact, if you use what you now see as "loneliness and singularity" to develop yourself into a whole person, you have much more to offer the world and will begin to see the whole world in a different way. Pain is merely something that helps you to understand. Listen to your body. Make peace with who you are by using mindfulness as your friend.

**Chapter 22: The Power Of Positivity**

Being positive simply allows you to have a shift in perspective. The Law of Correspondence says that everything within the Universe has a counterpart. This means that where there is negative, there is also positive but it is up to us as to which one we choose to see.

In this vibrational Universe, we are a match to the vibration we hold within us. If we are angry we will attract angry people and if we are happy we will attract happy people. This runs along the same stream as positive and negative. If we are in a positive head space then we see the positive in every situation but if we are in a negative head space, we will see the negative in every situation.

Why is it important to be Positive?

In order to live a life that we enjoy, we have to look for the positive as it is always there. You can achieve anything in life. You can go anywhere, be anybody, the world is your playground but only if you believe it is.

It is so important to be positive so that we get the best out of life. To be negative and to see out the negative, is exhausting. The reason it's exhausting is that it not only goes against the natural flow of the Universe, it also goes against the real us. We are not made of negative energy, we look for it. If we were to be totally ourselves, to be free of all the 'real world' problems and just be, we would naturally be positive.

How can positivity change your life?

When you only seek out the positive in things in your life then the positive things in life will seek out you. The Law of Perpetual Transmutation of Energy reminds us that we have the ability to change our entire life situation but just shifting our energy in the right direction. Everything on this earth is energy and where every is, energy goes. If we are focusing on having a lack of money then we will continue to have very little but if we can just focus on something more positive then the energy shall go there your life will start to change.

Be patient with yourself

The majority of us have been brought up to speak and think only of what is true in our current reality. For example, 'my car always goes wrong' or, 'money is always tight for me.' What many don't realize is that the more these things are said, the more prominent they get.

In order to turn your life around you must be patient with yourself as you learn to change your thoughts around. If you are used to pointing out negative things then you're naturally going to see them so be patient with yourself as you try to start seeing the positive.

Finding the positive in everything

Try to really look for that positive aspect because it is there. If you don't see it now, you will in the future. If you can, focus back to situations where something happened that was displeasing to you and from there, look at the positive things that came out of it. Even if there is just one, it is there. Then, focus purely on that rather than the negative as this will create a shift of energy.

Finding the bigger picture

Always look for the bigger picture. We may see little money in the account, negative people around us, an unfulfilling job, but what is the bigger picture? What are you learning? From having little money you are asking the Universe for more. From being around negative people you are creating a strong desire to be around happy people. From having an unfulfilling job you are naturally seeking out something much bigger. Life is a constant creative flow and we are always learning what to ask for next to make it more of what we want, we just have to see the bigger picture.

Simple Tips:

·Choose to look for the positive, even if it's small

·If something is displeasing, choose to focus on something else

·Be aware of the energy in others—is it positive or negative?

·Write down the positives in all the areas of your life

## Chapter 23: Overcoming Perfectionism

Are you a perfectionist? If you're trying to decide the best way to say yes, then you're a perfectionist. Little joke there; very little, but a joke. Okay, if you're a perfectionist, do you also procrastinate? And do you understand the link between procrastination and perfectionism?

Maybe I should state it differently, as the link between perfectionism and procrastination, because it is the perfectionism that leads to the procrastination.

So let's look at that.

The What: Most perfectionists procrastinate. There is a link. When you ask a perfectionist for a project, it will be exquisite when it's done, but it may not be done on time-in fact it probably won't be. Because...

The Why: Perfectionists are never done with anything. It has to be just right, and that means spending more time on it.

They don't procrastinate on purpose. I mean, we don't. But we do procrastinate because we're not satisfied with what we've done. We're always going for perfect, and that puts us behind. We don't know the meaning of good enough. That's why we put procrastination and perfectionism together.

Now, I'm going switch the How and the What If. You'll see why in a moment.

What If What if we could have a lower setting of perfectionism for things that do only have to be "good enough"? What if we didn't have to push ourselves so hard to get everything exactly right? How would that feel?

At first, it would feel pretty weird, but as we break the link between procrastination and perfectionism, we'd start to feel great. We'd realize we can do good work-even great work-on time if we can just relax our standards a little.

How: I'm not saying this is going to be easy, but again what if? What if we could lower our standards in one area, just one area, just for a week? Not drop our standards, but accept good enough. One small area for one week.

The evaluation and see how we're doing regarding procrastination and perfectionism and quality of work. Adjust as necessary, but be honest. Is it working out? If it's not, do something different, but if it's going okay, then expand it to another small area for another week.

Breaking the link between procrastination and perfectionism won't be an instant process. You will get frustrated and it will feel weird. But it's important that you try.

There are any number of "good" reasons and moral justifications for engaging in perfectionism, including:

We have an investment in being the best, single-handedly

We believe others do not share our same high standards

We believe others are incapable or unwilling to do the work we've been able to do.

We believe mistakes are unacceptable.

We believe our reputation is dependent upon being flawless.

We fear that the work will not get done if we don't stay and see it through.

We want to head off future problems by doing it ourselves; damage control.

Training is not a strong suit. It seems easier to do it ourselves than to muster the patience and take the time to teach.

One of the challenges we face is that our perfectionism is re-enforced by those around us who benefit from it. Customers and employers respect our follow-through, diligence, and that the job is always done perfectly and on time. This re-enforcement keeps our distortions about perfection alive and well. However, behind the facade of superiority lies a very painful truth: we believe if we are not perfect, we will not be accepted or appreciated, much less praised. Less is not acceptable. Without perfectionism, we will be judged as inferior.

Martyrs try to dominate by manipulating emotions, and they stifle creativity, joyfulness and the possibility of fulfillment for others. Even though the martyr voluntarily assumes responsibility for anything and everything, she feels bitter about having to carry the whole load.

When perfectionism is at the root of martyrdom, everyone involved feels the undertone of distrust. It doesn't take long before those we circumvent, shove aside, out-shine and out-pace begin to resent the perfectionist game we have mastered.

It may be difficult at the time to see the insidious way perfectionism robs us of any hope of personal freedom. The truth is, perfectionism is a silent killer in the workplace. Yes, the perfectionist may get the job done, but the impact of her behavior on others is devastating to morale, and her energy investment in trying to have total control is simply not sustainable. She ultimately burns out, loses her enthusiasm and becomes overwhelmed by the pressure to keep it all going.

The bottom line is--- perfectionism will always limit us. However, we do have alternatives to the debilitating compulsion to be perfect.

We can change the way we define the quality of our work. We can accept that there is a point of diminishing returns, where our massive investment simply does not net us a corresponding improvement in the result.

We can admit that we don't need to spoil our customers or employees at the sacrifice of our well-being and possibly our sanity. If the environment does not support this healthy, self-valuing shift, then we also have the choice to move on to a new endeavor and leave perfectionism behind.

Perfectionism can be overcome through awareness of the fear that fuels it. We can then get support in making more appropriate decisions. By facing our insecurities and fears of uncertainty, we will be able to make authentic, sustainable and fulfilling choices that still produce a high-quality result for those whom we serve.

## Chapter 24: Learning Mindfulness Meditation

This chapter is devoted to teaching you how to use mindfulness meditation to make your life more manageable. People are always so nervous when you mention the word "Meditation" and they see people sitting in awkward positions and imagine that they must do the same to achieve any kind of success in their meditation practice. However, it's not at all like you may have imagined.

There are several kinds of meditation that are practiced in the field of mindfulness. The idea of these practices is to take your mind off everything and that includes all the bad things that are happening in your life and your obligations. You need this kind of space in order to make your life easier to handle. If your workload is too heavy, what you tend to do is try to tackle everything at once and make yourself stressed. Instead, what mindfulness does is teach you to take one task at a time – be totally mindful of it and complete it – and then move onto another task.

Mindfulness meditation helps you to achieve this. How? Well, when you mind is too stressed and your thoughts are stretched to the limit, you don't give it the relaxation that it needs to find its own answers. If you have ever lost something and searched everywhere for it, then you may be able to see what freeing up the mind does. When you stop looking, you may have experienced your mind actually telling you out of the blue where that object is. This is because the subconscious needs time to work behind the scenes and can often solve your problems for you, without any effort needed on your part. Thus, when you meditate, you are giving your mind that little bit of space that it needs.

Some people meditate to reach a better understanding of life. Some do it to get closer to their spiritual self and some merely use meditation as a way to switch off the mind and allow it to relax. Whatever your reasons are for trying this method of relaxation, you need to do it properly so that you gain as much advantage from it as you can.

Preparing yourself for meditation

Preparation for meditation is as important as meditation itself. In fact, if you don't prepare, chances are that you won't really achieve much from your meditation practice. You need to be in clothing that isn't tight – as this tends to cause a distraction. It's also a good idea to meditate in a space within your home where you know you will be undisturbed and your meditation won't have any interruptions. That includes sounds. You may not know it but the constant noise of a TV set in the background can actually stress you because it's not allowing the mind to relax. You need no music, and although there is music that you can use during relaxation sessions, meditation depends on less stimuli so your room should be quiet and undisturbed.

You will need a cushion if you are fit enough to sit on the floor and bend your knees, crossing your legs over each other. This is just a beginner's position and there's no need to do a full Lotus position. If you are unfit, it's perfectly acceptable to meditate in a chair, provided that your back is straight and you are completely comfortable, though if you do manage the floor position, you can place the cushion under your behind so that the leg crossing is more comfortable.

You also place your hands somewhere where they can't fiddle. If you put your hands together, you are always tempted to move your hands and this isn't the object of the exercise. Thus place your hands on each knee with the palm facing upward. That will stop the temptation to itch your knee or move your hand. This position is purposeful and will stop you from being tempted to move during your meditation session.

Breathing in a particular way

In this book, we have discussed breathing elsewhere, but think of this as a new chapter and follow the instructions that we are going to give because this breathing exercise is what is used during meditation in the early stages. When you have more experience, you can follow the routine shown after this because you will have more power over your mind. For the time being, close your eyes to stop any kind of distraction. Since you have never meditated before, you are more likely to achieve good meditation practice in this way.

When you are completely comfortable, breathe in through your nose to the count of 6 and feel the air entering your body. It's a good idea not to think of anything but the air entering your body. At first you will find this hard to do, but every time that you are tempted to think of other things, you must go back to counting one again. Hold the breath for the count of 7 and then breathe out to the count of 8. At the end of the exhale, that counts as one.

You keep doing the same thing and every time that you reach the exhalation, you count upward from one to ten and then start back at one again.

The purpose of breathing in this way

When you breathe outwardly for one count more than inwardly, you are expelling excess oxygen from your body. What happens when you stress is that you are likely to have too much oxygen in your bloodstream and this makes stress even harder to cope with. People that have panic attacks, for example, have these because they have little control over their breathing. The purpose of breathing in this way is to relax the body and prepare it for the meditative process. You are emptying your mind of problems. You are not permitting bad thoughts to go through your mind and are replacing them with conscious thoughts about the way that you are breathing.

How long you should meditate

It's very unlikely that you will last much longer than about quarter of an hour when you first start to meditate. Don't push yourself to do more. You can increase this once you are better at meditation and are able to get thoughts out of your mind effectively. I tend to meditate for an hour every day and I find that it clears out my head and allows the subconscious to actually work on my problems. I was very surprised at the end of one session to come out of meditation and open my eyes and instantly see the answer to a problem that had puzzled me for weeks. The clarity with which you can see things once you have learned meditation and can sustain it is amazing.

## Chapter 25: Maintaining Mindfulness

The only Obstacle before Accomplishment is quitting too early to reach the Goal

Mindfulness Meditation

Witness the Miner digging for wealth, ending the search an inch from gold.

How often have we abandoned a pursuit when we should have stayed the course?

The mind is in constant motion by its very nature. We peer into the past and plan for the future all while pondering the present. The machinations of the modern age have only sped up this mental pace, fracturing our focus among the fruits of technology. We are so used to multitasking and shifting our attention that the moment we try to stop thinking, the mind makes attempts to frantically fill the emptiness.

Mindfulness Meditation does not counter this tendency. Instead the idea is to observe these thoughts and watch them without attachment or evaluation.

Approach the matters occurring in your mind as if happening before you on a movie screen.

This practice builds upon the breath and body awareness you will develop with the previous exercises. Start easy as you begin, a ten minute session will do just fine. Your postural muscles are used to comfy armchairs doing most of the work for them. Trying to meditate for a prolonged time before you are ready can easily make you annoyed or discouraged. Once you get comfortable with the practice, you can then extend the sitting time. Gradually progress in increments of 5 minutes, going from 10 to 15 to 20.

1) First sit in a comfortable position on the floor or on a yoga mat. You can place a cushion or folded blanket under your pelvis to make sitting straight easier. Adjust the height of the cushion to your needs.

2) Place your palms above your knees. Straighten your spine, lift your sternum, and roll your shoulders back so they are

closer together. Relax the muscles in your back and your shoulders. Let go of all the tension.

3) Bring your attention to your breath and observe the sensations of inhaling and exhaling. Feel the motion of the air as it moves in and out of your nose. Follow the expansion and contraction of your chest as you continue breath awareness for a few minutes.

4) While remaining aware of your breath, expand your awareness to your entire body. Feel its position, find the rhythm of your pulse and identify every sensation that you can. Do not to move or react to external stimuli. Simply observe and retain your state of calm.

5) Next you will sense the space around you without opening your eyes. Focus your attention on what can you hear and feel in your setting. Do not judge or classify these sensations, acknowledge them as they come and go.

6) Various thoughts will pass through your mind in the calm and quite moments of this exercise. Observe them as well without attaching to any or getting carried away by your stream of consciousness. Remember to remain within the perspective of the witness; do not invest emotion into any fleeting thought. Calmly watch their constant movement as they rise and fall like the tide of the ocean.

7) Slowly open your eyes and sit in silence. Reflect on the serenity of the session.

In order to benefit from mindfulness practice it is best to do it every day. It is better to meditate for 10 minutes daily than to sit for an hour once a week. Mindful practice will become an unconscious habit that you can perform effortlessly. Early in the morning works best for many as the mind has not filled itself with the impressions of the day. Meanwhile the evening is preferable to others since it is a relaxing routine closer to day's end. Find the time that works best for you and stay consistent with your practices daily.

If you notice that your mind begins to wander, gently bring it back to center by observing the breath. Then expand your awareness back to your bodily sensation and thoughts. The key is to keep your awareness open and attentive, but not reactive or inspective.

It is not advisable to use an alarm clock for this exercise. An alarm will bring you out of the Mindfulness state in a very aggressive way. It is good however to use a timer to keep track of the length of your sessions.

Remember, you don't need to sit for a long time in the beginning. You don't want your Mindfulness practices to become another chore. Keep it pleasant and make it the part of the day that is just for you. Start with shorter times and extend the practice when you are ready. Again, consistency is the key to success! Simply keep in mind that practice makes perfect and you will progress as you continue to train.

## Conclusion

It is hoped that this book has given you food for thought. The way forward is to use some of the methods demonstrated within your life and to see how they improve your outlook and make your life worthwhile.

In the Buddhist religion, each person is accountable for their own mistakes. Thus, when someone is badly behaved toward you, you need to train yourself to understand that they need your empathy, rather than your anger. They have the problem, rather than you. The world is filled with so much negativity and blame and taking responsibility for your moment, your body, your spiritual awakening is all that you can do. Every human being is an island, a place where self responsibility and awareness is of paramount importance and we owe it to ourselves to be the very best person that we can be.

By following the mindful route, you do just that. You give yourself the best of each moment and, in doing so, give others the best of who you can be. This makes life a very comfortable place to be, where problems can be solved and where you can learn to live in harmony with others and with your own thoughts. That helps you to reach your potential, both physically and spiritually, as mindfulness is the tool given to everyone so that they can live worthwhile and satisfying lives, at peace with others and particularly with themselves.

If you are finding all of this a little hard to do, take on one part at a time and achieve one exercise. Once you see the benefits of that one exercise, it will naturally lead to the inner need to carry on and perform many more. These exercises help you to develop and it is hoped that they will also help you to move beyond bad moments in your life and to use these simply as a tool for learning to be empathetic with others feeling those same negative thoughts. Use each moment of your life to make it count. The most humble of people has the strongest voice in the wilderness of the world because they demand nothing and are totally aware of the moment in which they find themselves. Thus, you can incorporate these ideas yourself and find out how they enhance the way that you think and the way that you choose to live the life you have.

www.ingramcontent.com/pod-product-compliance
Lightning Source LLC
Chambersburg PA
CBHW072002070526
44583CB00015B/1301